History & Geography 1100
Teacher's Guide

W9-CBB-658

CONTENTS

Author:
Editor:

Alpha Omega Publications
Alan Christopherson, M.S.

Alpha Omega Publications®

804 N. 2nd Ave. E., Rock Rapids, IA 51246-1759
© MM by Alpha Omega Publications, Inc.   All rights reserved.
LIFEPAC is a registered trademark of Alpha Omega Publications, Inc.

CURRICULUM

OVERVIEW

HISTORY & GEOGRAPHY

Curriculum Overview
Grades 1–12

History & Geography LIFEPAC Overview

	Grade 1	Grade 2	Grade 3
LIFEPAC 1	**I AM A SPECIAL PERSON** • God made me • You are God's child • All about you • Using proper manners	**FAMILIES AND NEIGHBORS** • We need a family • We help our family • Our neighborhood • Helping our neighbors	**FISHING IN MAINE** • At look at Deer Island • A lobster boat • Planting lobster traps • Catching lobsters
LIFEPAC 2	**COMMUNICATING WITH SOUND** • Sounds people make • Sounds that communicate • Communicating without sound • Communicating with God	**COMMUNITY HELPERS** • What is a community • Community helpers • Your church community • Helping your community	**FARMING IN KANSAS** • The six parts of Kansas • Getting to know Kansas • Exploring Kansas • Harvest in Kansas
LIFEPAC 3	**I HAVE FEELINGS** • I feel sad • I feel afraid • I feel happy • I have other feelings	**NEIGHBORHOOD STORES** • Pioneer goods and services • Modern goods and services • Some business rules • God's business rules	**FRUIT-GROWING IN WASHINGTON** • Geography of Washington • Cities in Washington • Apple blossom time • Apple harvest time
LIFEPAC 4	**I LIVE IN A FAMILY** • My mother and father • My brothers and sisters • My grandparents • What my family does	**FARMS AND CITIES** • Farming long ago • Farming today • Growing cities • Changing cities	**FORESTS IN OREGON** • A land of forests • Trees of the forests • Lumbering in Oregon • Keeping Oregon's forests
LIFEPAC 5	**YOU AND GOD'S FAMILY** • Getting ready in the morning • Walking to school • The school family • The church family	**NEIGHBORS AROUND THE WORLD** • Things all families need • How communities share • How communities change • Customs of the world	**CALIFORNIA: A GOLDEN LAND** • Early California • The ranch community • A trip around the state • Work on a truck farm
LIFEPAC 6	**PLACES PEOPLE LIVE** • Life on the farm • Life in the city • Life by the sea	**A JAPANESE FAMILY** • Places people live in Japan • School in Japan • Work in Japan • Play in Japan	**CATTLE IN TEXAS** • Learning about Texas • Early ranches in Texas • Life on a ranch • A cattle round-up
LIFEPAC 7	**COMMUNITY HELPERS** • Firemen and policemen • Doctors • City workers • Teachers and ministers	**HOW WE TRAVEL** • Travel in Bible times • Travel in the past • Travel today • Changes in today's world	**COAL MINING IN PENNSYLVANIA** • The formation of coal • Products from coal • Methods of mining coal • The state of Pennsylvania
LIFEPAC 8	**I LOVE MY COUNTRY** • America discovered • The Pilgrims • The United States begin • Respect for your country	**MESSAGES FROM FAR AND NEAR** • Communication in Bible times • Communication today • Reasons for communication • Communication without sound	**MANUFACTURING IN MICHIGAN** • Facts about Michigan • Interesting people of Michigan • Places in Michigan • The treasures in Michigan
LIFEPAC 9	**I LIVE IN THE WORLD** • The globe • Countries • Friends in Mexico • Friends in Japan	**CARING FOR OUR NEIGHBORHOODS** • God's plan for nature • Sin changed nature • Problems in our neighborhoods • Helping our neighborhoods	**SPACE TRAVEL IN FLORIDA** • A place to launch spacecraft • Worker at the Space Center • The first flights • The trip to the moon
LIFEPAC 10	**THE WORLD AND YOU** • You are special • Your family • Your school and church • Your world	**PEOPLE DEPEND ON EACH OTHER** • Depending on our families • Depending on our neighbors • Depending on our communities • Communicating with God	**REVIEW OF NINE STATES** • California and Kansas • Washington and Maine • Oregon and Pennsylvania • Texas, Florida and Michigan

Grade 4	Grade 5	Grade 6	
OUR EARTH • The surface of the earth • Early explorations of the earth • Exploring from space • Exploring the oceans	**A NEW WORLD** • Exploration of America • The first colonies • Conflict with Britain • Birth of the United States	**WORLD GEOGRAPHY** • Latitude and longitude • Western and eastern hemispheres • The southern hemisphere • Political and cultural regions	LIFEPAC 1
SEAPORT CITIES • Sydney • Hong Kong • Istanbul • London	**A NEW NATION** • War for independence • Life in America • A new form of government • The nation's early years	**THE CRADLE OF CIVILIZATION** • Mesopotamia • The land of Israel • The Nation of Israel • Egypt	LIFEPAC 2
DESERT LANDS • What is a desert? • Where are the deserts? • How do people live in the desert?	**A TIME OF TESTING** • Louisiana Purchase • War of 1812 • Sectionalism • Improvements in trade & travel	**GREECE AND ROME** • Geography of the region • Beginning civilizations • Contributions to other civilizations • The influence of Christianity	LIFEPAC 3
GRASSLANDS • Grasslands of the world • Ukraine • Kenya • Argentina	**A GROWING NATION** • Andrew Jackson's influence • Texas & Oregon • Sectionalism • Improvements in trade & travel	**THE MIDDLE AGES** • The feudal system • Books and schools • The Crusades • Trade and architecture	LIFEPAC 4
TROPICAL RAIN FORESTS • Facts about rain forests • Rain forests of the world • The Amazon rain forest • The Congo rain forest	**A DIVIDED NATION** • Civil War • Reconstruction • Gilded Age • The need for reform	**SIX SOUTH AMERICAN COUNTRIES** • Brazil • Colombia • Venezuela • Three Guianas	LIFEPAC 5
THE POLAR REGIONS • The polar regions: coldest places in the world • The Arctic polar region • The Antarctic polar region	**A CHANGING NATION** • Progressive reforms • Spanish-American War • World War I • Roaring Twenties	**OTHER AMERICAN COUNTRIES** • Ecuador and Peru • Bolivia and Uruguay • Paraguay and Argentina • Chile	LIFEPAC 6
MOUNTAIN COUNTRIES • Peru – the Andes • The Incas and modern Peru • Nepal – the Himalayas • Switzerland – the Alps	**DEPRESSION AND WAR** • The Great Depression • War begins in Europe • War in Europe • War in the Pacific	**AFRICA** • Geography and cultures • Countries of northern Africa • Countries of central Africa • Countries of southern Africa	LIFEPAC 7
ISLAND COUNTRIES • Islands of the earth • Cuba • Iceland • Japan	**COLD WAR** • Korean War & other crises • Vietnam War • Civil Rights Movement • Upheaval in America	**MODERN WESTERN EUROPE** • The Renaissance • The Industrial Revolution • World War I • World War II	LIFEPAC 8
NORTH AMERICA • Geography • Lands, lakes and rivers • Northern countries • Southern countries	**INTO THE NEW MILLENNIUM** • Watergate and détente • The fall of Communism • The Persian Gulf • Issues of the new millennium	**MODERN EASTERN EUROPE** • Early government • Early churches • Early countries • Modern countries	LIFEPAC 9
OUR WORLD IN REVIEW • Europe and the explorers • Asia and Africa • Southern continents • North America, North Pole	**THE UNITED STATES OF AMERICA** • Beginning America until 1830 • Stronger America 1830-1930 • 1930 to the end of the millennium • The new millennium	**THE DEVELOPMENT OF OUR WORLD** • Cradle of civilization • The Middle Ages • Modern Europe • South America and Africa	LIFEPAC 10

History & Geography LIFEPAC Overview

	Grade 7	Grade 8	Grade 9
LIFEPAC 1	**WHAT IS HISTORY** • Definition and significance of history • Historians and the historical method • Views of history	**EUROPE COMES TO AMERICA** • Voyages of Columbus • Spanish exploration • Other exploration • The first colonies	**UNITED STATES HERITAGE** • American colonies • Acquisitions and annexations • Backgrounds to freedom • Backgrounds to society
LIFEPAC 2	**WHAT IS GEOGRAPHY** • Classes of geography • Geography and relief of the earth • Maps and the study of our world • Time zones	**BRITISH AMERICA** • British colonies • Government • Lifestyle • Wars with France	**OUR NATIONAL GOVERNMENT** • Ideals of national government • National government developed • Legislative and Executive branches • Judicial branch
LIFEPAC 3	**U.S. HISTORY AND GEOGRAPHY** • Geography of the U.S. • Early history of the U.S. • Physical regions of the U.S. • Cultural regions of the U.S.	**THE AMERICAN REVOLUTION** • British control • Rebellion of the Colonies • War for independence • Constitution	**STATE AND LOCAL GOVERNMENT** • Powers of state government • County government • Township government • City government
LIFEPAC 4	**ANTHROPOLOGY** • Understanding anthropology • The unity of man • The diversity of man • The culture of man	**A FIRM FOUNDATION** • Washington's presidency • Adams administration • Jeffersonian Democracy • War of 1812	**PLANNING A CAREER** • Definition of a career • God's will concerning a career • Selecting a career • Preparation for a career
LIFEPAC 5	**SOCIOLOGY** • Sociology defined • Historical development • Importance to Christians • Method of sociology	**A GROWING NATION** • Jacksonian Era • Northern border • Southern border • Industrial Revolution	**CITIZENSHIP** • Citizenship defined • Gaining citizenship • Rights of citizenship • Responsibilities of citizenship
LIFEPAC 6	**U.S. ANTHROPOLOGY** • Cultural background of the U.S. • Native American cultures • Cultures from distant lands • Cultural and social interaction	**THE CIVIL WAR** • Division & Secession • Civil War • Death of Lincoln • Reconstruction	**THE EARTH AND MAN** • Man inhabits the earth • Man's home on the earth • Man develops the earth • The future of the earth
LIFEPAC 7	**ECONOMICS** • Economics defined • Methods of the economist • Tools of the economist • An experiment in economy	**GILDED AGE TO PROGRESSIVE ERA** • Rise of industry • Wild West • America as a world power • Progressive era	**REGIONS OF THE WORLD** • A region defined • Geographic and climate regions • Cultural and political regions • Economic regions of Europe
LIFEPAC 8	**POLITICAL SCIENCE** • Definition of political science • Roots of Western thought • Modern political thinkers • Political theory	**A WORLD IN CONFLICT** • World War I • Great Depression • New Deal • World War II	**MAN AND HIS ENVIRONMENT** • The physical environment • Drug abuse • The social environment • Man's responsibilities
LIFEPAC 9	**STATE ECONOMICS AND POLITICS** • Background of state government • State government • State finance • State politics	**COLD WAR AMERICA** • Origins of the Cold War • Vietnam • Truman to Nixon • Ending of the Cold War	**TOOLS OF THE GEOGRAPHER** • The globe • Types of maps • Reading maps • The earth in symbol form
LIFEPAC 10	**SOCIAL SCIENCES REVIEW** • History and geography • Anthropology • Sociology • Economics and politics	**RECENT AMERICA & REVIEW** • Europe to independence • Colonies to the Civil War • Civil War to World War II • World War II through Cold War	**MAN IN A CHANGING WORLD** • Development of the nation • Development of government • Development of the earth • Solving problems

Grade 10	Grade 11	Grade 12	
ANCIENT CIVILIZATION • Origin of civilization • Early Egypt • Assyria and Babylonia • Persian civilization	FOUNDATIONS OF DEMOCRACY • Democracy develops • Virginia • New England colonies • Middle and southern colonies	INTERNATIONAL GOVERNMENTS • Why have governments • Types of governments • Governments in our world • Political thinkers	LIFEPAC 1
ANCIENT CIVILIZATIONS • India • China • Greek civilization • Roman Empire	CONSTITUTIONAL GOVERNMENT • Relations with England • The Revolutionary War • Articles of Confederation • Constitution of the U.S.	UNITED STATES GOVERNMENT • U.S. Constitution • Bill of Rights • Three branches of government • Legislative process	LIFEPAC 2
THE MEDIEVAL WORLD • Introduction to Middle Ages • Early Middle Ages • Middle Ages in transition • High Middle Ages	NATIONAL EXPANSION • A strong federal government • Revolution of 1800 • War of 1812 • Nationalism and sectionalism	AMERICAN PARTY SYSTEM • American party system • Development political parties • Functions of political parties • Voting	LIFEPAC 3
RENAISSANCE AND REFORMATION • Changes in government and art • Changes in literature and thought • Advances in science • Reform within the Church	A NATION DIVIDED • Issues of division • Division of land and people • Economics of slavery • Politics of slavery	HISTORY OF GOVERNMENTS • Primitive governments • Beginnings of Democracy • Feudalism, Theocracy & Democracy • Fascism & Nazism	LIFEPAC 4
GROWTH OF WORLD EMPIRES • England and France • Portugal and Spain • Austria and Germany • Italy and the Ottoman Empire	A NATION UNITED AGAIN • Regionalism • The division • The Civil War • Reconstruction	THE CHRISTIAN & GOVERNMENT • Discrimination & the Christian • Christian attitudes • "Opinion & Truth" in politics • Politics & Propaganda	LIFEPAC 5
THE AGE OF REVOLUTION • Factors leading to revolution • The English Revolution • The American Revolution • The French Revolution	INVOLVEMENT AT HOME & ABROAD • Surge of industry • The industrial lifestyle • Isolationism • Involvement in conflict	FREE ENTERPRISE • Economics • Competition • Money through history • International finance & currency	LIFEPAC 6
THE INDUSTRIAL REVOLUTION • Sparks of preparation • Industrial revolution in England • Industrial revolution in America • Social changes of the revolution	THE SEARCH FOR PEACE • The War and its aftermath • The Golden Twenties • The Great Depression • The New Deal	BUSINESS AND YOU • Running a business • Government & business • Banks & Mergers • Deregulation & Bankruptcy	LIFEPAC 7
TWO WORLD WARS • Mounting tension • World War I • Peace and power quests • World War II	A NATION AT WAR • Causes of the war • World War II • Korean Conflict • Vietnam Conflict	THE STOCK MARKET • How it started and works • Selecting stocks • Types of stocks • Tracking stocks	LIFEPAC 8
THE CONTEMPORARY WORLD • The Cold War • Korean War and Vietnam War • Collapse of the Soviet Union • Today's world	CONTEMPORARY AMERICA • America in the 1960s • America in the 1970s • America in the 1980s & 90s • International Scene 1980-Present	BUDGET AND FINANCE • Cash, Credit & Checking • Buying a car • Grants, Loans & IRAs • Savings & E-cash	LIFEPAC 9
ANCIENT TIMES TO THE PRESENT • Ancient civilizations • Medieval times • The Renaissance • The modern world	UNITED STATES HISTORY • Basis of democracy • The 1800s • Industrialization • Current history	GEOGRAPHY AND REVIEW • Euro & International finance • U.S. Geography • The global traveler • Neighbors, Heroes & The Holy Land	LIFEPAC 10

LIFEPAC

MANAGEMENT

11

STRUCTURE OF THE LIFEPAC CURRICULUM

The LIFEPAC curriculum is conveniently structured to provide one teacher handbook containing teacher support material with answer keys and ten student worktexts for each subject at grade levels two through twelve. The worktext format of the LIFEPACs allows the student to read the textual information and complete workbook activities all in the same booklet. The easy to follow LIFEPAC numbering system lists the grade as the first number(s) and the last two digits as the number of the series. For example, the Language Arts LIFEPAC at the 6th grade level, 5th book in the series would be LAN0605.

Each LIFEPAC is divided into 3 to 5 sections and begins with an introduction or overview of the booklet as well as a series of specific learning objectives to give a purpose to the study of the LIFEPAC. The introduction and objectives are followed by a vocabulary section which may be found at the beginning of each section at the lower levels, at the beginning of the LIFEPAC in the middle grades, or in the glossary at the high school level. Vocabulary words are used to develop word recognition and should not be confused with the spelling words introduced later in the LIFEPAC. The student should learn all vocabulary words before working the LIFEPAC sections to improve comprehension, retention and reading skills.

Each activity or written assignment has a number for easy identification, such as 1.1. The first number corresponds to the LIFEPAC section and the number to the right of the decimal is the number of the activity.

Teacher checkpoints, which are essential to maintain quality learning, are found at various locations throughout the LIFEPAC. The teacher should check 1) neatness of work and penmanship, 2) quality of understanding (tested with a short oral quiz), 3) thoroughness of answers (complete sentences and paragraphs, correct spelling, etc.), 4) completion of activities (no blank spaces) and 5) accuracy of answers as compared to the answer key (all answers correct).

The self test questions are also number coded for easy reference. For example, 2.015 means that this is the 15th question in the self test of Section II. The first number corresponds to the LIFEPAC section, the zero indicates that it is a self test question and the number to the right of the zero the question number.

The LIFEPAC test is packaged at the centerfold of each LIFEPAC. It should be removed and put aside before giving the booklet to the student for study.

Answer and test keys have the same numbering system as the LIFEPACs and appear at the back of this handbook. The student may be given access to the answer keys (not the test keys) under teacher supervision so that he can score his own work.

A thorough study of the Curriculum Overview by the teacher before instruction begins is essential to the success of the student. The teacher should become familiar with expected skill mastery and understand how these grade level skills fit into the overall skill development of the curriculum. The teacher should also preview the objectives that appear at the beginning of each LIFEPAC for additional preparation and planning.

TEST SCORING and GRADING

Answer keys and test keys give examples of correct answers. They convey the idea, but the student may use many ways to express a correct answer. The teacher should check for the essence of the answer, not for the exact wording. Many questions are high level and require thinking and creativity on the part of the student. Each answer should be scored based on whether or not the main idea written by the student matches the model example. "Any Order" or "Either Order" in a key indicates that no particular order is necessary to be correct.

Most self tests and LIFEPAC tests at the lower elementary levels are scored at 1 point per answer; however, the upper levels may have a point system awarding 2 to 5 points for various answers or questions. Further, the total test points will vary; they may not always equal 100 points. They may be 78, 85, 100, 105, etc.

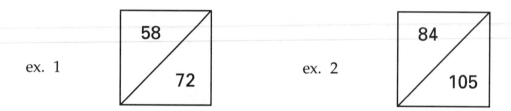

ex. 1   58 / 72   ex. 2   84 / 105

A score box similar to ex.1 above is located at the end of each self test and on the front of the LIFEPAC test. The bottom score, 72, represents the total number of points possible on the test. The upper score, 58, represents the number of points your student will need to receive an 80% or passing grade. If you wish to establish the exact percentage that your student has achieved, find the total points of his correct answers and divide it by the bottom number (in this case 72.) For example, if your student has a point total of 65, divide 65 by 72 for a grade of 90%. Referring to ex. 2, on a test with a total of 105 possible points, the student would have to receive a minimum of 84 correct points for an 80% or passing grade. If your student has received 93 points, simply divide the 93 by 105 for a percentage grade of 89%. Students who receive a score below 80% should review the LIFEPAC and retest using the appropriate Alternate Test found in the Teacher's Guide.

The following is a guideline to assign letter grades for completed LIFEPACs based on a maximum total score of 100 points.

LIFEPAC Test = 60% of the Total Score (or percent grade)
Self Test   = 25% of the Total Score (average percent of self tests)
Reports   = 10% or 10* points per LIFEPAC
Oral Work   = 5% or 5* points per LIFEPAC
*Determined by the teacher's subjective evaluation of the student's daily work.

Example:

LIFEPAC Test Score	=	92%	92	x	.60	=	55 points
Self Test Average	=	90%	90	x	.25	=	23 points
Reports						=	8 points
Oral Work						=	4 points

TOTAL POINTS   =   90 points

Grade Scale based on point system:

100	–	94	=	A
93	–	86	=	B
85	–	77	=	C
76	–	70	=	D
Below		70	=	F

TEACHER HINTS and STUDYING TECHNIQUES

LIFEPAC Activities are written to check the level of understanding of the preceding text. The student may look back to the text as necessary to complete these activities; however, a student should never attempt to do the activities without reading (studying) the text first. Self tests and LIFEPAC tests are never open book tests.

Language arts activities (skill integration) often appear within other subject curriculum. The purpose is to give the student an opportunity to test his skill mastery outside of the context in which it was presented.

Writing complete answers (paragraphs) to some questions is an integral part of the LIFEPAC Curriculum in all subjects. This builds communication and organization skills, increases understanding and retention of ideas and helps enforce good penmanship. Complete sentences should be encouraged for this type of activity. Obviously, single words or phrases do not meet the intent of the activity, since multiple lines are given for the response.

Review is essential to student success. Time invested in review where review is suggested will be time saved in correcting errors later. Self tests, unlike the section activities, are closed book. This procedure helps to identify weaknesses before they become too great to overcome. Certain objectives from self tests are cumulative and test previous sections; therefore, good preparation for a self test must include all material studied up to that testing point.

The following procedure checklist has been found to be successful in developing good study habits in the LIFEPAC curriculum.

1. Read the introduction and Table of Contents.
2. Read the objectives.
3. Recite and study the entire vocabulary (glossary) list.
4. Study each section as follows:
    a. Read the introduction and study the section objectives.
    b. Read all the text for the entire section, but answer none of the activities.
    c. Return to the beginning of the section and memorize each vocabulary word and definition.
    d. Reread the section, complete the activities, check the answers with the answer key, correct all errors and have the teacher check.
    e. Read the self test but do not answer the questions.
    f. Go to the beginning of the first section and reread the text and answers to the activities up to the self test you have not yet done.
    g. Answer the questions to the self test without looking back.
    h. Have the self test checked by the teacher.
    i. Correct the self test and have the teacher check the corrections.
    j. Repeat steps a–i for each section.

5. Use the SQ3R* method to prepare for the LIFEPAC test.
6. Take the LIFEPAC test as a closed book test.
7. LIFEPAC tests are administered and scored under direct teacher supervision. Students who receive scores below 80% should review the LIFEPAC using the SQ3R* study method and take the Alternate Test located in the Teacher Handbook. The final test grade may be the grade on the Alternate Test or an average of the grades from the original LIFEPAC test and the Alternate Test.

> *SQ3R: **S**can the whole LIFEPAC.
> **Q**uestion yourself on the objectives.
> **R**ead the whole LIFEPAC again.
> **R**ecite through an oral examination.
> **R**eview weak areas.

GOAL SETTING and SCHEDULES

Each school must develop its own schedule, because no single set of procedures will fit every situation. The following is an example of a daily schedule that includes the five LIFEPAC subjects as well as time slotted for special activities.

Possible Daily Schedule

8:15	–	8:25	Pledges, prayer, songs, devotions, etc.
8:25	–	9:10	Bible
9:10	–	9:55	Language Arts
9:55	–	10:15	Recess (juice break)
10:15	–	11:00	Mathematics
11:00	–	11:45	Social Studies
11:45	–	12:30	Lunch, recess, quiet time
12:30	–	1:15	Science
1:15	–		Drill, remedial work, enrichment*

*Enrichment: Computer time, physical education, field trips, fun reading, games and puzzles, family business, hobbies, resource persons, guests, crafts, creative work, electives, music appreciation, projects.

Basically, two factors need to be considered when assigning work to a student in the LIFEPAC curriculum.

The first is time. An average of 45 minutes should be devoted to each subject, each day. Remember, this is only an average. Because of extenuating circumstances a student may spend only 15 minutes on a subject one day and the next day spend 90 minutes on the same subject.

The second factor is the number of pages to be worked in each subject. A single LIFEPAC is designed to take 3 to 4 weeks to complete. Allowing about 3-4 days for LIFEPAC introduction, review and tests, the student has approximately 15 days to complete the LIFEPAC pages. Simply take the number of pages in the LIFEPAC, divide it by 15 and you will have the number of pages that must be completed on a daily basis to keep the student on schedule. For example, a LIFEPAC containing 45 pages will require 3 completed pages per day. Again, this is only an average. While working a 45 page LIFEPAC, the student may complete only 1 page the first day if the text has a lot of activities or reports, but go on to complete 5 pages the next day.

Long range planning requires some organization. Because the traditional school year originates in the early fall of one year and continues to late spring of the following year, a calendar should be devised that covers this period of time. Approximate beginning and completion dates can be noted on the calendar as well as special occasions such as holidays, vacations and birthdays. Since each LIFEPAC takes 3-4 weeks or eighteen days to complete, it should take about 180 school days to finish a set of ten LIFEPACs. Starting at the beginning school date, mark off eighteen school days on the calendar and that will become the targeted completion date for the first LIFEPAC. Continue marking the calendar until you have established dates for the remaining nine LIFEPACs making adjustments for previously noted holidays and vacations. If all five subjects are being used, the ten established target dates should be the same for the LIFEPACs in each subject.

FORMS

The sample weekly lesson plan and student grading sheet forms are included in this section as teacher support materials and may be duplicated at the convenience of the teacher.

The student grading sheet is provided for those who desire to follow the suggested guidelines for assignment of letter grades found on page 3 of this section. The student's self test scores should be posted as percentage grades. When the LIFEPAC is completed the teacher should average the self test grades, multiply the average by .25 and post the points in the box marked self test points. The LIFEPAC percentage grade should be multiplied by .60 and posted. Next, the teacher should award and post points for written reports and oral work. A report may be any type of written work assigned to the student whether it is a LIFEPAC or additional learning activity. Oral work includes the student's ability to respond orally to questions which may or may not be related to LIFEPAC activities or any type of oral report assigned by the teacher. The points may then be totaled and a final grade entered along with the date that the LIFEPAC was completed.

The Student Record Book which was specifically designed for use with the Alpha Omega curriculum provides space to record weekly progress for one student over a nine week period as well as a place to post self test and LIFEPAC scores. The Student Record Books are available through the current Alpha Omega catalog; however, unlike the enclosed forms these books are not for duplication and should be purchased in sets of four to cover a full academic year.

WEEKLY LESSON PLANNER

Week of:

	Subject	Subject	Subject	Subject
Monday				
	Subject	Subject	Subject	Subject
Tuesday				
	Subject	Subject	Subject	Subject
Wednesday				
	Subject	Subject	Subject	Subject
Thursday				
	Subject	Subject	Subject	Subject
Friday				

WEEKLY LESSON PLANNER

Week of:

	Subject	Subject	Subject	Subject
Monday				
	Subject	Subject	Subject	Subject
Tuesday				
	Subject	Subject	Subject	Subject
Wednesday				
	Subject	Subject	Subject	Subject
Thursday				
	Subject	Subject	Subject	Subject
Friday				

Student Name _____   Year _____

Bible

LP #	Self Test Scores by Sections 1	2	3	4	5	Self Test Points	LIFEPAC Test	Oral Points	Report Points	Final Grade	Date
01											
02											
03											
04											
05											
06											
07											
08											
09											
10											

History & Geography

LP #	Self Test Scores by Sections 1	2	3	4	5	Self Test Points	LIFEPAC Test	Oral Points	Report Points	Final Grade	Date
01											
02											
03											
04											
05											
06											
07											
08											
09											
10											

Language Arts

LP #	Self Test Scores by Sections 1	2	3	4	5	Self Test Points	LIFEPAC Test	Oral Points	Report Points	Final Grade	Date
01											
02											
03											
04											
05											
06											
07											
08											
09											
10											

Student Name _____   Year _____

Mathematics

LP #	Self Test Scores by Sections 1	2	3	4	5	Self Test Points	LIFEPAC Test	Oral Points	Report Points	Final Grade	Date
01											
02											
03											
04											
05											
06											
07											
08											
09											
10											

Science

LP #	Self Test Scores by Sections 1	2	3	4	5	Self Test Points	LIFEPAC Test	Oral Points	Report Points	Final Grade	Date
01											
02											
03											
04											
05											
06											
07											
08											
09											
10											

Spelling/Electives

LP #	Self Test Scores by Sections 1	2	3	4	5	Self Test Points	LIFEPAC Test	Oral Points	Report Points	Final Grade	Date
01											
02											
03											
04											
05											
06											
07											
08											
09											
10											

NOTES

INSTRUCTIONS FOR HISTORY & GEOGRAPHY

The LIFEPAC curriculum from grades two through twelve is structured so that the daily instructional material is written directly into the LIFEPACs. The student is encouraged to read and follow this instructional material in order to develop independent study habits. The teacher should introduce the LIFEPAC to the student, set a required completion schedule, complete teacher checks, be available for questions regarding both content and procedures, administer and grade tests and develop additional learning activities as desired. Teachers working with several students may schedule their time so that students are assigned to a quiet work activity when it is necessary to spend instructional time with one particular student.

The Teacher Notes section of the Teacher's Guide lists the required or suggested materials for the LIFEPACs and provides additional learning activities for the students. The materials section refers only to LIFEPAC materials and does not include materials which may be needed for the additional activities. Additional learning activities provide a change from the daily school routine, encourage the student's interest in learning and may be used as a reward for good study habits.

ADDITIONAL LEARNING ACTIVITIES

Section I Foundation of the American Republic

1. How much likelihood is there that exploration and colonization might have begun in Europe under the conditions of a medieval society? What kind of things had to change in order that exploration might become widespread? What kind of changes had to come about to make colonization possible?

2. Do you agree with the concept that the crusades were a catalyst for exploration of lands beyond European shores? Can you describe the sequence set in motion by the crusades which made exploration possible?

3. How much of a factor do you think the Reformation was in the "Age of Discovery"? Did the breakdown of papal authority contribute to the emergence of another form of authority which, in turn, aided the "Age of Discovery"?

4. Work up a scenario with Marco Polo as the key figure. Let Polo visit three typical groups of medieval society: noblemen, serfs and clergy. Polo should urge each group to follow his example and establish a program for discovery of the still "unknown" world. Each group's response should identify the limitations or impossibilities to the challenge because of the structure of society.

5. Stage a series of "before" and "after" vignettes, putting the following characters opposite one another: serfs and noblemen; noblemen and kings; kings and clergy. The "before" should be prior to the Renaissance. The dialogue should indicate the difference in the relationship between characters as a result of the breakdown and transformation of society.

6. Let a student research the matter of the connection between the crusades and colonization thoroughly enough that he might write a substantive "domino theory" paper on the topic.

7. The transformation from feudal society to nation-states in Europe is not well defined. Let a student research the era and write a graphic account of the change. Perhaps he could do this activity by a series of lapsed time sketches centering on the life of a serf, a nobleman and a king.

Section II Colonization Begins

1. Was the failure of the Roanoke Colony a vital step toward colonial expansion into the New World? Why did the New World present problems neither Africa nor India had? How did joint-stock companies spring from the Roanoke failure?

2. Were the charter, royal and proprietary colonies linked to differing trends and pressures in England? Explain.

3. How might you specify the area of difference between the Pilgrims and the Puritans? What was the relationship of these groups to the British government? Did the Pilgrims and the Puritans ever clash with one another?

4. Have the students work in small groups to research problems of the Puritans and Pilgrims. The groups may then script a short play to be presented as a drama before the class or as a puppet show.

5. A student may read *The Light and the Glory* by Peter Marshall, then write a short essay entitled, "Did God Have a Plan for America?"

6. Students may read Puritan literature, such as Anne Bradstreet's or Edward Taylor's poetry; Jonathan Edward's conversion narrative or his sermon ("Sinners in the Hands of an Angry God"); or perhaps portions of Captain John Smith's *Description of New England*, William Bradford's *History of Plymouth Plantation*, or William Byrd's *History of the Dividing Line* or his *Secret Diary*. These selections may be readily found in an anthology of colonial writing. The teacher should carefully screen any suggested anthologies for unacceptable selections before making them available to the students.

Section III Middle and Southern Colonies

1. Do you believe the three colonial types (charter, royal, proprietary) could have been equally effective in any of the thirteen colonies? What specific problems did each solve?

2. Given the history of the Separatists in England, do you find it surprising that Rhode Island would have been the first colony to grant blanket religious freedom?

3. What kind of generalizations can you make about the following subjects:
   a. nationality of the leadership in the colonies
   b. life-style in the colonies
   c. motives for settlement of the colonies

   Is it safe to say that the colonists were influenced by the European system to maintain isolation from one another?

4. What in your opinion were the three most significant events in the growth of the European civilizations on the eastern seaboard of America?

5. Have a panel of five students discuss the most democratic colonial principles incorporated into the United States Constitution.

6. Have a student prepare a research paper contrasting and comparing life in the middle colonies to life in the southern colonies.

7. Suggest that a student make a relief map of the original thirteen colonies depicting the physical features such as rivers, bays, inlets, lakes, mountains, the piedmont and coastal plain areas. Have him include the fall line and any other features he may care to incorporate.

8. Have several students choose favorite characters (Anne Hutchinson, William Penn, Roger Williams, or John Smith), research their lives, then be interviewed by an on-the-spot reporter.

ADDITIONAL LEARNING ACTIVITIES

Section I Relations with Britain

1. Assist the students in finding copies of the Mayflower Compact. Trace ideas that were passed down to the Declaration of Independence and the Constitution.

2. Read aloud excerpts from Thomas Paine's *Common Sense.* Discuss which ideas are to be found incorporated into the Constitution.

3. Take the class to a museum to see early Indian or colonial exhibits.

4. Have several students stage a town meeting to discuss what action they (as colonists) plan to take against the unfair taxation imposed by the British.

5. Have a student report on Patrick Henry's role in the colonists' quest for independence.

Section II The Revolutionary War

1. Have the students make a record of the progress of the war on a map of the middle and southern colonies.

2. Discuss the hardships endured by Washington and his men at Valley Forge. Have students draw or paint their impressions of Valley Forge following the discussion.

3. Have a student take the part of a favorite Revolutionary leader, research his part in the war, then be interviewed by a classmate as an "on-the-scene" reporter.

Section III Birth of a Nation

1. Discuss the weaknesses of the Articles of Confederation and how the document might have been strengthened.

2. Read aloud the Preamble of the Constitution. Discuss the values and need for having a preamble. Lead the students in listing their own ideas for what should be included if they were to write such a document. Then using their own ideas and their own words, work to write a Preamble on the chalkboard, involving the entire class.

3. Have two groups of students debate the adoption of the Constitution from the points of view of Massachusetts and Virginia.

4. Have the student draw a political cartoon or cartoons dealing with the problems involved in the ratification of the Constitution.

ADDITIONAL LEARNING ACTIVITIES

Section I Ship of State

1. Have students count off by two's to form two groups. Direct students to take out paper and pencil and have teams list answers to your questions derived from the first five objectives (i.e., identify four major parts of Hamilton's financial plan).

2. The students could be divided into three small groups: Federalists, Republicans and newsmen. Party members should familiarize themselves with the appropriate party philosophy, while newsmen should be acquainted with both sides in order to interview the members. Panel-type interviews may be held before the rest of the class in an effort to compare basic philosophies.

3. A student may wish to prepare a chart comparing the views of the Federalists and Republicans on specific issues grouped under such headings as federal-state relations, economic affairs and foreign policy.

Section II The Revolution of 1800 and War of 1812

1. After reviewing the elements of debate with the students, the teacher may assign the following topics to small groups which will, at an assigned time, present their prepared debate before the class:
    a. the *Marbury v. Madison* decision
    b. the effectiveness of a trade embargo
    c. the inevitability of the War of 1812

2. A small group of students may construct a relief map of the Louisiana Purchase territory. This project could easily be adapted to an individual project.

3. A student may wish to construct a time line listing the main events of the administrations of Washington and Adams.

4. On an outline map of the United States, students may show how the territory of the United States had expanded by 1800.

5. A student may prepare a report to present to the class about the Lewis and Clark Expedition. Include a map of their travels and tell about their activities along the way. Use encyclopedias or other resource material from the school library or public library in preparing the report. Include some original cartoons, charts, poetry or other creative writing. A tape recorder, overhead transparencies or other audio-visual methods to present a part or all of the report may be used.

6. Jefferson wanted to be remembered for founding the University of Virginia and for drafting the Declaration of Independence and the Virginia Statute of Religious Liberty. What conclusions do you draw from this expressed preference? Present your views about Jefferson in a brief editorial that might have been published in an American newspaper following Jefferson's death on July 4, 1826. You might want to read from other sources about Jefferson's life before completing this activity.

7. Draw a cartoon dealing with one of these subjects:
    a. XYZ Affair
    b. impressment of American seamen
    c. feeling of Westerners about New Orleans
    d. Hamilton's financial plan

8. When western farmers balked at paying the tax on whiskey, the government mobilized 13,000 men to enforce the law. In what ways was this situation comparable (or not comparable) to the colonists' refusal to pay the Stamp Tax? Write your answer to be submitted for extra credit.

Section III Nationalism and Sectionalism

1. Have students collect news items referring to the Monroe Doctrine. Students may either use the *New York Times Index*, finding references to the Doctrine in that newspaper, then using the date as a means of finding the citation within a local or regional newspaper, or they may collect references throughout the allotted study period for this LIFEPAC.

2. Small groups may research the factions for and against the National Bank during the 1830s, then present their findings to the class as an oral report.

3. Students may research one aspect of the Western movement, then present their findings to the class. Students may enjoy an independent study of the "real West" or the "real cowboy" vs. the Hollywood or Madison Avenue stereotype. Other aspects might include investigation of sourdough baking (with a sharing of the results) or canning or food preservation techniques (fruit leather or beef jerky). Students may interview their grandparents, trying to find information about their own family's possible Western migration.

ADDITIONAL LEARNING ACTIVITIES

Section I A Nation Divided

1. Using wall maps, have students point out the three components of the Missouri Compromise.

2. Form two *small* groups comprised of no more that five students. Have each group take one side of the Missouri Compromise, research it, then make a conversation-style presentation of their findings.

3. Students may wish to study further one of the major land acquisitions: The Louisiana Purchase, the Gadsden Purchase, or the Mexican Cession. They may draw maps of the territory, including pictures of resources typically found in that area and thereby adding resources to the United States.

Section II Slavery

1. Suggest several books that may be read for extra credit or for independent study or book reports. If you wish, all members of the class may give oral book reports on books dealing with slavery. Some suggestions include these books:

    Percy, William A. *Lanterns on the Levee: Recollections of a Planter's Son.* New York: Alfred A. Knopf, Inc., 1941.

    Stowe, Harriet B. *Uncle Tom's Cabin.* New York: MacMillan Publishing Co., 1962.

    Before making assignments, teachers should be thoroughly familiar with the material to be sure books do not contain objectionable material.

2. Small groups may collect news items suggesting that slavery still has effects today and that, in fact, not all issues of the Civil War have been resolved. Material may be shared with the class in brief oral reports and then class discussion.

3. Students may wish to write poems, short stories, songs, one-act plays or essays about their feelings toward and experiences with slavery and racial prejudice. You may wish to have a class discussion first about prejudices—toward short people, blondes, smart people, rich people, poor people, artists, athletes and so forth. The idea that each of us has experienced some form of prejudice will probably be introduced. A writing assignment may then be made.

ADDITIONAL LEARNING ACTIVITIES

Section I Regional Lifestyles

1. Have various students map out in class the expansion of America from 1800 to 1860. Date each acquisition as territory and each territory as it became a state. Once the map is complete, color in the seceding states one color, the Union states another. Compare this final map with a modern one.

2. Stage in class a mock congressional debate concerning the issues of secession and slavery. Assign certain students to defend the South, others to support the Northern unionists and abolitionist causes. If they wish, students may research some of the actual congressional debates of the 1850s before holding their own mock session.

3. Have each student read a teacher-approved biography of one of the historical figures of the Civil War period and prepare to answer questions on his choice in class.

Section II Civil War

1. Divide the class into several groups and assign each group a specific Civil War battle. Give them a few days for research and then have each group present a detailed report on their battle for the class. (Suggestions: maps of troop positions, statistics on the number of troops involved, the kind of battle, types of weapons, casualties—are all facts that should be included.)

2. Have each student make a Civil War portfolio that includes pictures of the troops and battles, sketches or photographs of the weapons, portraits of the leading figures of the War (soldiers and politicians) and so forth. Set aside a day when these portfolios can be brought to class and shared.

Section III Reconstruction

1. Divide the class into three groups and assign each group one of the following amendments: Thirteenth, Fourteenth and Fifteenth. Each group should obtain a copy of their amendment and prepare to discuss it in class. Include in these discussions the applications of these amendments for us today.

2. Have each student choose one of the following topics and prepare a brief oral report on that choice for the class.
   a. Black Codes
   b. Republican radicals
   c. Carpetbaggers
   d. Johnson's impeachment
   e. Ku Klux Klan
   f. Poll taxes and literacy tests

3. Lead a class discussion concerning the following hypothetical question: Would Reconstruction in the South have been less harsh had Lincoln lived? If so, why? Encourage class participation in the debate.

ADDITIONAL LEARNING ACTIVITIES

Section I U.S. Industry

1. Lead a class discussion concerning the new methods of transportation and communication developed in the nineteenth century. Bring out the effects these new methods had on industry.

2. Ask the class the question: What advantages did factories have over earlier home workshops? List the points brought out on the board. (Example: would today's society be possible without mass production?)

3. Schedule a class field trip to a modern factory. Have the students observe production techniques and hold a brief class discussion after the trip.

4. Have the students chart, locate and identify America's natural resources on a map of this country.

5. Have each student draw or construct a model of one of the early inventions that aided industry.

Section II Industrial Life Style

1. Lead a class discussion on one of the following topics.

   a. Factors leading to the birth of the labor movement
   b. The dangers arising when corporations form monopolies

2. Arrange for a corporation president (or the head of any large business in your area) to address the class on the procedures and structure of his business.

3. Have a union spokesman address the class concerning the problems of workers today.

4. Read a teacher-approved biography of an industrial tycoon and make an oral report to the class.

5. Make a chart covering the various levels of authority in a corporation, from owner to factory worker. If possible, research a real corporation.

Section III Foreign Policy

1. Organize a class discussion concerning the Panama Canal that covers the following issues

   a. What advantages did the canal bring America in the beginning?
   b. What advantages does America enjoy from it today? What disadvantages?
   c. What will be the result of turning the canal over to Panama?

2. Invite a local senior citizen to address the class on their recollections of the earlier part of this century.

3. If possible, obtain and show in class a film documenting the building of the Panama Canal or Teddy Roosevelt's life.

4. Chart present American possessions and protectorates on a global map.

5. Chart on a map of Panama the canal's route and location of all its levels. Identify the area ceded to Panama by the United States.

Section IV March toward Conflict

1. Try to obtain and show in class a film on prewar Europe that illustrates the rising tension there.

2. Divide the class into three groups and assign each group of the following topics: nationalism, capitalism and imperialism. Give each a few days to research their topic and then have each group present a report to the class.

3. Map prewar Europe, showing the positions of the Alliance and Entente countries. Compare this map with a modern one. How many of those pre-1914 countries exist today?

ADDITIONAL LEARNING ACTIVITIES

Section I The Great War and Its Aftermath

1. Obtain and show the class a film of either World War I, the peace meetings in Versailles or the presidency of Woodrow Wilson. Hold a class discussion afterward on the film.

2. Divide the class into three groups and give each group a global map. Have one group chart and identify the nations of the world as they existed in 1914. Let the second group do the same with the nations of the world in 1936 just prior to World War II. Then have the third group chart the world as it is today. Compare these three maps in class.

3. Have each student outside of class read a teacher-approved biography on one of the major figures of this period in history (World War I and the two postwar decades). Written reports are not necessary, but students should be able to give a brief oral summary to the class and answer any questions about their book.

Section II The Golden Twenties

1. Organize a class discussion concerning prohibition in America. Encourage the students to state their opinions and to support those opinions with facts.

2. There are a number of newsreel films, documentaries and books about the life style of the Twenties. If a film is available, show it to the class. If not, choose a book (or books) that is well illustrated (including clothing, cars, fads, etc.) and share it with the class. Discuss the differences and similarities in that life style and that of today.

3. As a follow-up to the preceding activity, have each student pick a particular phase of the Twenties' life style and compile a portfolio of data on that phase. (Example: fashion or music) When they are completed, share the portfolios with the entire class.

Section III The Great Depression

1. If a video is available, show it to the class. If not, substitute books, newspapers and magazines of that era (the Great Depression) and share them with the class.

2. Invite a senior citizen who lived through the Depression to address the class on the conditions of those times. Afterward hold a question and answer session and encourage the students to question the speaker.

3. Have each student list the causes of the Depression in what he considers the order of their importance. Let the students bring their lists to class and compare them. Are any of those factors present in our economy today? Is another depression of that magnitude possible? Encourage discussion of this point.

Section IV The New Deal

1. The New Deal did more to change the lives of Americans and the function of government than any other single program in our history. Go over in class the most important accomplishments of that program, accenting the ones that affect Americans today in particular.

2. First show a film about the life of Franklin Roosevelt or, if a film is unavailable, share a biography of him with the class. Then organize a class discussion or debate on the statement: Roosevelt was the right man at the right time; only a president like him could have pulled America out of the depression. (hint: Some historians credit Roosevelt with America's recovery; others claim World War II, not the president, saved America from economic chaos.) Give the students a few days to research their subject before holding the debate.

3. Have each student write a brief biography of Franklin D. Roosevelt, using this LIFEPAC and other sources for their research. A two-page limit is suggested.

ADDITIONAL LEARNING ACTIVITIES

Section I World War II

1. Have various students map out in class (possibly on the board) the step-by-step American takeover on the Pacific front.

2. Lead a class discussion concerning the economic status of the world before World War II, with particular emphasis on the Great Depression and its effects in America and Europe.

3. Divide the class in half and organize a debate concerning the atomic bombing of Japan. (Make one side pro, the other con.)

4. Obtain and view in class a film of interviews with World War II veterans. Lead a class discussion reviewing differing roles of soldiers in the war. Also discuss the soldiers' views of the importance of their contribution to the defense of freedom in the world.

5. Have each student select and read a teacher-approved biography of one of the historical figures of World War II (Hitler, Eisenhower, Rommel, Churchill, etc.) Each student should prepare an oral report for the class.

6. Have students collect sketches, photographs and drawings of World War II military equipment and make a portfolio. (If time permits, set aside a class period during which these portfolios can be passed around and shared.)

Section II Korean Conflict

1. Organize a class discussion comparing and contrasting the League of Nations and the United Nations.

2. Show a film on the organization of the United Nations, the Korean conflict or the life of Eisenhower.

3. Invite participants of the Korean conflict to share their experiences with the class.

4. Label on a map of the world the Communist-controlled countries, the Free or Democratic nations and the neutral (sometimes called Third World) powers during the Cold War.

5. Read a teacher approved biography of Mao, Chiang, Eisenhower, Kennedy, Johnson and so forth. Prepare a brief oral report for the class.

Section III Vietnam Conflict

1. List and discuss in class the crises of Kennedy's presidency.

2. List and discuss in class the problems that arose in America as a direct result of this nation's involvement in Vietnam.

3. Show in class a documentary film on Vietnam—the fighting, the withdrawal or the return of the POW's. Then hold a class discussion of the film.

4. Chart the early satellites of the space race, including nationality, accomplishment and value.

5. Interview a Vietnam veteran and present an oral report of your findings to the class.

ADDITIONAL LEARNING ACTIVITIES

Section I America in the 1960s

1. Show a film on one of the following subjects and afterwards hold a class discussion of the film:
   a. John F. Kennedy
   b. The Civil Rights movement
   c. The early American space program
   d. The Vietnam War controversy
   e. Martin Luther King

2. Invite one of the following people to address the class and participate in a question-and-answer session with the students:
   a. a civil rights worker
   b. a representative of the space program (or former representative)
   c. a former member of the Peace Corps

3. Research and list all the Civil Rights legislation and court decisions since 1954.

4. Johnson brought about the passage of much legislation for his Great Society. Locate a copy of any one of the bills passed and read it to the class. (Example: voting rights law, federal aid to education, new housing laws)

5. Turn the class into a mock legislature for a day and debate passage of any one of the bills of the Great Society. Assign certain students to introduce the bill and support it, others to oppose and argue against it. The remainder of the class should be neutral. After the debate call for a vote and determine which side won.

6. Interview an adult in your community about his reaction to Kennedy's assassination. Questions could include (1) What were you doing when you learned of Kennedy's death? (2) How did you react to Johnson's taking over the presidency?

Section II America in the 1970s

1. Only two presidents were ever impeached in office, Andrew Johnson and Bill Clinton, who were both found not guilty by the House of Representatives. Look up the details and share them with the class. Discuss the similarities and differences between those and President Nixon's case.

2. Trace the progress of America's space program from 1960 until the early seventies. A chart of this progress might best illustrate this advancement.

3. Divide the class into two groups and debate one of the following topics:
   a. SALT
   b recognition of China
   c. Détente
   d. the pardon of Richard Nixon
   e. Busing
   f. the American reaction to the invasion of Afghanistan

4. On a map of Southeast Asia, chart the history of that area, beginning with the French domination before World War II and ending with the present day. (Include the Japanese in World War II, the French afterwards, their withdrawal, the division of Indochina, etc.)

5. Write a paper on one of these topics:
   a. The Iran Hostage Crisis
   b. The *Mayaguez* rescue
   c. American economic problems from 1970 to 2000

Section III American in the 1980s and 1990s

1. Learn your parents' opinions on one of these topics and report back to the class.
    a. Reaganomics
    b. Endangered Species Act
    c. Iran-Contra Affair
    d. Political activism by Christians
    e. NAFTA
    f. AIDS
    g. The presidency of Ronald Reagan
    h. The presidency of Bill Clinton

2. As a class, research and make a list of the advantages to the United States from the space shuttle program.

3. Write a paper on the abortion issue from 1973 to the present day.

4. Write a brief report on a national Christian organization giving its objectives and methods. Possibilities include: The National Right to Life, The Christian Coalition, Focus on the Family, Promise Keepers and Operation Rescue.

5. Research and write an opinion paper on why you believe or do not believe your education is better than one you would receive at your local public school.

6. Go over in class, for review purposes, the step-by-step process through which Ford became president. Explain how this process proves that the Constitution does work. (Many other nations could have resorted to revolution and violence in such a situation. Instead, America underwent an orderly transfer of power.)

7. Organize a class debate over President Ford's granting amnesty to the Vietnam dissenters. Encourage all the students to participate. If possible, support the points with Biblical references.

8. Inflation is a problem that began in President Nixon's administration, continued and is present today. To illustrate this problem, make a list of any ten items, record the price of that item today and through research, find out the price of that same item in 1969. Exchange completed lists with other students and compare pricing.

Section IV The International Scene 1980 - 2000

1. Make a time line of the fall of communism.

2. Make a list of the acts of terrorism against Americans, including the group responsible for the act (if known) from 1970 to 2000. Discuss.

3. Have a Persian Gulf War veteran speak to the class.

4. Research and write a paper on the ethnic divisions and problems in the former Yugoslavia.

5. Research and debate the U.S. invasions of Grenada and Panama. Were these further misuses of the Monroe Doctrine?

ADDITIONAL LEARNING ACTIVITIES

Section I Foundations of Democracy

1. After reading aloud excerpts from journals kept during the crossing or by Captain John Smith, you may ask students to examine and through discussion or drama re-create the fears, pressures and hopes felt by early colonists.

2. After reading aloud excerpts from journals kept during the crossing or by Captain John Smith, you may ask students to re-create and express in writing the fears, pressures and hopes felt by early colonists by composing a diary, simulating the crossing experience or the first year of settlement, drawing from other historical accounts.

3. Several students may write to the chamber of commerce in Williamsburg and in Boston to secure information about the reconstruction of these cities. Groups may wish to plan a hypothetical visit to one of these areas, collecting information that could be used on a sightseeing expedition.

Section II Beginnings of United States Democracy/Revolutionary War

1. Read selections to the students from Benjamin Franklin's *Autobiography,* especially the section stating his plan for self-improvement. The students may wish to design their own plans; approach this activity cautiously, gauging the interest and response of your class. The activity would be futile if the class did not approach it seriously.

2. Groups of students may build relief models of major Revolutionary War battles. If they prefer, they could draw maps and color the battlegrounds.

3. Students may research the biographies of Revolutionary heroes and heroines, looking for some people who are often overlooked in history textbooks. The students may write a brief biographical sketch about the person. If desired, portraits could be drawn.

Section III United States of the 1800s

1. Using large wall maps, have students point out major battles of the Civil War. Students may research a particular battle, then give brief, oral reports in connection with the map exercise.

2. Students may wish to research battles of the Civil War. Excellent accounts were written by Daniel Aaron and Shelby Foote. Relief models of battlegrounds may be designed or students may draw and color area maps depicting the battlegrounds.

3. Students may examine the biographies of Jefferson, Monroe, Jackson and Lincoln, choosing one president to research and study. Then, at an assigned time, the students may share their information with the class in a brief, oral report.

Section IV Industrialization of the United States

1. Make arrangements for students to tour a local factory. Students should be prepared to ask the tour guides questions about wages, unions, working hours, employee safeguards and so forth. When the class returns from the tour, compare and contrast nineteenth-century working conditions with those of a similar industry today.

2. Have small groups of students play Monopoly, Master Mind, Easy Money, Risk, or Stock Market, or other profit–motivated games. They may wish to invent their own games, based on the same motif.

3. Students may wish to "buy" stock, then keep track of their company and its profits through *The Wall Street Journal* over a brief period. Oral reports may be shared with the class after a specified amount of time.

Section V The United States: Roosevelt to Clinton

1. Make arrangements to take your class to the state capitol for a day. Contact your local representative or senator to ensure your choosing an interesting session (although even a dull one may be used to good educational purposes).

2. After touring the capitol building and perhaps meeting state politicians and listening to a day in the legislature, have students give short, group reports on various aspects of the tour. These aspects will vary widely, depending upon the tour itself.

3. Students may wish to become involved with either a presidential campaign or with a local political campaign. Encourage students to share their experiences with the class.

Section VI Current Events

1. Follow a controversial event in the newspaper for several weeks. Then, write a letter to the editor of your local paper about your opinion of it.

2. Visit NASA's website and get information on a recent shuttle mission. Discuss its importance in class.

3. As a class, formulate a foreign policy for a newly elected president.

4. As a class, make up your own political party and write a platform for it.

T
E
S
T
S

Reproducible Tests
for use with the History &
Geography 1100 Teacher's
Guide

Name _____

Write *true* or *false* (each answer, 1 point).

1. _____ Marco Polo traveled around the Far East and then to Africa.

2. _____ The progress of learning brought enormous pressure on the medieval structure of life.

3. _____ The mercantile theory called for a surplus of export over import.

4. _____ The House of Burgesses was part of the first democratic government in the colony of Virginia.

5. _____ The colony in which religious freedom for all was permitted was Massachusetts.

6. _____ The Mayflower Compact was a treaty signed by the Indians.

7. _____ The religious group that disagreed with the established Church of England was called the Puritans.

8. _____ The first English colonies proved that no venture could succeed without royal favor and businesslike planning.

9. _____ The Pilgrims were Puritans who settled in Plymouth in 1620.

10. _____ The system of indenture helped solve economic problems in England.

Write the letter for the correct answer on each line (each answer, 2 points).

11. The crusades did *not* _____ .
    a. create a demand for Eastern goods
    b. rescue the Holy Land permanently from the Muslims
    c. bring about the breakdown of the medieval way of life
    d. cause cities and towns to grow larger and wealthier

12. During the medieval period the Catholic Church _____ .
    a. stood by the side of the kings
    b. avoided an involvement with the crusades
    c. united the diverse people of Europe with a common identity
    d. supported the Reformation

13. The Renaissance _____ .
    a. contributed to the strengthening of the manorial system
    b. was strengthened by the invention of the printing press
    c. had nothing to do with the invention of scientific instruments
    d. began in Germany

14. The first Englishman to attempt to colonize what is now the U.S. was _____ .
    a. John Rolfe   c. John Smith
    b. Sir Walter Raleigh d. William Penn

15. A colonist who agreed to work for another in return for passage to America was called _____ .
   a. a settler   c. an indentured servant
   b. an adventurer   d. burgess

16. The first Englishman to attempt to grow tobacco in the New World was _____ .
   a. John Rolfe   c. Roger Williams
   b. Sir Walter Raleigh   d. John Smith

17. The first Englishman to sail around the world was _____ .
   a. Sir Francis Drake   c. John Cabot
   b. Sir Walter Raleigh   d. James Oglethorpe

18. Englishman became interested in colonies through the efforts of the geographer, _____ .
   a. John Rolfe   c. John Cabot
   b. Richard Hakluyt   d. John Smith

19. Maryland was the first _____ .
   a. Quaker colony   c. colony to grant full religious freedom
   b. Catholic colony   d. colony to be taken over by the duke of York

Match these items (each answer, 2 points).

20. _____ first written constitution in the colonies   a. Pennsylvania

21. _____ tidewater and piedmont   b. Pilgrims

22. _____ Separatists   c. colony owned by an individual

23. _____ William Penn   d. Carolina

24. _____ proprietary   e. Georgia

25. _____ Oglethorpe   f. fall line

                                                            g. Fundamental Orders of Connecticut

Complete these statements (each answer, 3 points).

26. The colony that was established in Virginia in 1607 was _____ .

27. The man who took New York from the Dutch was the _____ .

28. John Winthrop was the leader of the _____ colony.

29. Many Catholics settled in the colony of _____ .

30. Those colonists seeking complete religious freedom settled in _____ .

31. Thomas Hooker founded the colony of _____ .

32. The colony of Delaware was a _____ colony.

33. The Carolinas were governed by _____ proprietors.

34. Pennsylvania was settled by the _____ .

35. James Oglethorpe was the leader of the colony of _____ .

```
 56
────
 70
```

Score
Teacher Check _____

Initial   **Date**

History & Geography 1102 Alternate Test

Name _____

Write *true* or *false* (each answer, 1 point).

1. _____ George Grenville planned to put Britain's finances in order after the French and Indian War by revising and enforcing American customs duties and regulations.

2. _____ The colonists were shocked by the denial of their rights as Englishmen.

3. _____ The Stamp Act Congress of 1765 appointed George Washington as commander of the Continental Army.

4. _____ When the British sent troops to Boston in 1768, the colonists declared war.

5. _____ Samuel Adams led the effort to establish the committees of correspondence.

6. _____ The Intolerable Acts taught the colonists that parliamentary supremacy meant an end to the power of their own assemblies.

7. _____ At Bunker Hill the British learned that the Americans' fighting power had been underestimated.

8. _____ The Second Continental Congress of 1775 conducted America's first central government.

9. _____ The First Continental Congress met in response to the Intolerable Acts.

Complete these statements (each answer, 3 points).

10. Calling for republican government, _____ said that common sense forbade American loyalty to the king.

11. The man concerned with making the colonial militia into a Continental army and with finding supplies for the army was _____ .

12. The battle of Saratoga convinced the _____ to help America.

13. In the 1778 Alliance between the United States and France, France resolved to help the United States win its _____ .

14. The French fleet helped the American cause in the battle of _____ .

15. The 1783 Treaty of Paris provided that the United States was to be a free and independent state with _____ as its western boundary.

16. The principles of equality expressed in the Declaration of Independence had almost no effect upon the issue of _____ .

17. Supporters of the new Constitution in 1787 were called _____ .

18. One of the first controversial issues faced by the young republic was control of _____ .

19. A strong central government was not provided for in the _____ .

20. Territorial expansion of the nation was guided by provisions of the _____ of 1787.

Answer these questions (each answer, 5 points).

21.   What was a major early obstacle at the 1787 Constitutional Convention?

_____

_____

_____

_____

22.   What important personal guarantees were not included in the Constitution.

_____

_____

_____

_____

23.   What did opponents of the Constitution fear and oppose?

_____

_____

_____

24.   Explain the terms of the "Great Compromise."

_____

_____

_____

_____

_____

Match these items (each answer, 2 points).

25. _____ Loyalist
26. _____ George Washington
27. _____ Thomas Jefferson
28. _____ James Madison
29. _____ Benedict Arnold
30. _____ General Cornwallis
31. _____ Thomas Paine
32. _____ John Paul Jones
33. _____ Nathan Hale
34. _____ George Rogers Clark

a. proposed separate branches of government
b. *Common Sense*
c. proposed the Virginia Plan
d. secured the western lands
e. American spy who gave his life
f. led the Constitutional Convention
g. author of Declaration of Independence
h. British general who surrendered at Yorktown
i. Tory
j. betrayed his country
k. famous naval hero

Complete these activities (each answer, 5 points).

35. Name three weaknesses of the Articles of Confederation.

   a. _____

   _____

   b. _____

   _____

   c. _____

   _____

36. Name the three branches into which the federal government was divided by the Constitution.

   a. _____

   b. _____

   c. _____

90/112

Score
Teacher Check _____

Initial   Date

Name _____

Write *true* or *false* (each answer, 1 point).

1. _____ Part of Alexander Hamilton's financial program was to protect the state banking system.

2. _____ The followers of Alexander Hamilton held that the Constitution should be loosely interpreted.

3. _____ Jay's Treaty did not provide that the British would stop impressing American seamen and interfering with American trade.

4. _____ Pinckney's Treaty with Spain guaranteed U.S. navigation rights on the Mississippi River.

5. _____ The Alien and Sedition Acts were proposed by both Republicans and Federalists.

6. _____ The Jefferson administration did not eliminate the Federalists' policies and programs.

7. _____ Jefferson believed that the government should not be a burden to anyone.

8. _____ The War of 1812 was a war of many contradictions.

9. _____ The Treaty of Ghent solved none of the causes of the War of 1812.

10. _____ During the "Era of Good Feelings," sectional trends were beginning to form.

Complete this activity (each answer, 3 points).

11. The major points of the Monroe Doctrine were
    a. _____
    b. _____
    c. _____
    d. _____

Complete these statements (each answer, 3 points).

12. As each section of the country developed into either an industrial or an agricultural area, sectional differences _____ .

13. The Jacksonian Era saw the advancement of democratic policies begun during the _____ .

14. Washington established a group of advisors from the government department heads called the _____ .

15. The first political parties were formed as a result of the split between a. _____ b. _____ and c. _____ .

16. To alleviate the possibility of another election like the ones of 1796 and 1800, the _____ was passed.

17. The Louisiana Purchase was explored by _____ .

18.   President Jefferson believed in a _____ to meet the needs of an agrarian society.

19.   The War Hawks wanted to declare war on _____ .

20.   The section that wanted western expansion with slavery was the _____ .

21.   The first secretary of the treasury was _____ .

22.   The political party headed by Jefferson and Madison was called the _____

23.   The opposing party, headed by Hamilton, was called the _____ .

24.   A separate vote for the president and vice president was required by the _____ to the Constitution.

25.   From the standpoint of American morale, the war that was a "Second War of Independence" was the _____

26.   "Clinton's Big Ditch," connecting Albany and Buffalo, is better known as the

_____ .

27.   The agreement that allowed a particular state to be admitted to the union as a slave state and a northern state admitted as a free state in 1820 is known as the _____ .

28.   The awarding of public offices to political supporters is called the_____ .

Match these items (each answer, 2 points).

29.   _____   XYZ Affair

30.   _____   Monroe Doctrine

31.   _____   Jay's Treaty

32.   _____   Louisiana Purchase

33.   _____   Alien and Sedition Acts

34.   _____   the Chesapeake Affair

35.   _____   Embargo Acts of 1807

a. brought the problem of impressment to a head

b. criticized by both parties as being unconstitutional

c. involved the United States and France

d. fixed the boundary between the United States and West Florida at the 31st parallel

e. closed all American ports to foreign ships to sail to any foreign ports

f. stated that the British would turn over forts along the Great Lakes to the United States

g. became a landmark of American doctrine

h. initiated by Napoleon

Name _____

Write *true* or *false* (each answer, 2 points).

1. _____ The most frequent method of resistance by black people to slavery was sabotage.

2. _____ Economic reasons alone caused sectionalism to develop.

3. _____ Sojourner Truth was an abolitionist.

4. _____ Simon Legree led United States troops into California.

5. _____ Santa Anna led the Mexican army against the Texans at the Alamo.

6. _____ Harriet Tubman wrote *Uncle Tom's Cabin*.

7. _____ Chief Justice Taney ruled in the *Marbury vs. Madison* case.

8. _____ Jim Bowie led the raid on Harper's Ferry.

9. _____ John Brown was a leading conductor for the underground railroad.

10. _____ Daniel Webster opposed state rights and nullification.

Complete these statements (each answer, 4 points).

11. The second state added to the Union as a result of the Missouri Compromise was

_____ .

12. The general subject of the Lincoln-Douglas debates was _____ .

13. The specific subject of the Lincoln-Douglas debates was _____ .

14. Three categories of slave labor found on plantations were a. _____ ,
b. _____ and c. _____ .

15. An anti-slavery newspaper was the _____

16. The Compromise of 1850 was proposed by _____ .

17. People in the west wanted tariff money used to build _____ .

18. The Wilmont Proviso would have forbidden slavery in _____ .

19. The U.S. and Britain agreed to divide _____ on the 49th parallel.

20. The state of _____ began as a Spanish, then Mexican, territory and was an independent republic for ten years before joining the Union.

21. The most hated part of the Compromise of 1850 in the north was the _____ .

Match these items (each answer, 4 points).

22. _____ manifest destiny   a. helped repeal the Missouri Compromise indirectly

23. _____ suffrage   b. freedman abolitionist

24. _____ popular sovereignty   c. became a political martyr

25. _____ tariff   d. freed from slavery

26. _____ Dred Scott case   e. expand from Atlantic to the Pacific

27. _____ Frederick Douglass   f. tax

28. _____ John Brown   g. right to vote

     h. squatters rights

$\frac{80}{100}$

Score

Teacher Check

_____

Initial   Date

Name _____

Write *true* or *false* (each answer, 1 point).

1. _____ The first battle of the Civil War was at Fort Sumter.

2. _____ Poll taxes were part of Northern Reconstruction.

3. _____ Samuel Morse invented the telegraph.

4. _____ New Orleans was captured by Grant.

5. _____ The South had more resources for raw materials than the North during the Civil War.

6. _____ Money to finance the Civil War was obtained by the Morrill Tariff in the North.

7. _____ Lincoln abolished slavery during the Civil War.

8. _____ By 1860 slavery had existed in America for two hundred years.

9. _____ The institution of slavery helped progress in the South.

10. _____ The Ku Klux Klan opposed black civil rights.

Match these items (each answer, 2 points).

11. _____ George McClellan

12. _____ Freedman's Bureau

13. _____ Republican radicals

14. _____ John Wilkes Booth

15. _____ South Carolina

16. _____ Alexander H. Stephens

17. _____ Manifest Destiny

18. _____ Robert E. Lee

19. _____ agrarian

20. _____ Major Robert Anderson

21. _____ George Meade

22. _____ Georgia

a. advocated harsh reconstruction

b. first state to secede

c. Union general, good organizer

d. won at Chancelorville and Seven Days

e. helped black people after the Civil War

f. killed Lincoln

g. farming economy

h. vice president of the Confederacy

i. idea that America should stretch from ocean to ocean

j. devastated by William T. Sherman

k. victorious general at Gettysburg

l. Union commander of Fort Sumter

m. Jefferson Davis

Write the letter for the correct answer on each line (each answer, 2 points).

23. The president during the Civil War was _____ .
    a. Andrew Jackson   c. Andrew Johnson
    b. Abraham Lincoln   d. Stephen Douglas

24. The most important crop to the South was _____ .
    a. cotton   c. wheat
    b. rice   d. corn

25. Vicksburg was captured by _____ .
    a. Farragut   c. Grant
    b. Lee   d. Johnson

26. The amendment to the United States Constitution that abolished slavery was the _____ .
    a. fifteenth   c. ninth
    b. sixteenth   d. thirteenth

27. New England manufacturing was protected from competition of cheap British goods by the
    _____ of 1816.
    a. protective tariff   c. taxes
    b. embargo   d. strong navy

28. Southerners opposed the election of Lincoln because of his stand _____ .
    a. for the industrial north   c. to immediately abolish slavery
    b. on the protective tariff   d. against slavery

29. The South surrendered to Grant at _____ .
    a. Richmond   c. Vicksburg
    b. Appomattox   d. Washington

30. The president of the Confederacy was _____ .
    a. Henry Clay   c. Jefferson Davis
    b. Andrew Johnson   d. Stephen Douglas

31. The senator who proposed a compromise after the South seceded was _____ .
    a. Alexander Stephens   c. John Crittenden
    b. Winfield Scott   d. Stephen Douglas

32. Prior to the Civil War the Southern class structure was dominated by the _____ .
    a. planters   c. merchants
    b. military   d. artisans

Complete these statements (each answer, 3 points).

33. The Radical Republican law that forbade the president to dismiss cabinet members as the

    _____ .

34. Northerners who came south to find business opportunities during Reconstruction were called

    _____ .

35. The man who won the 1876 presidential election was _____ even though
    b. _____ had the most votes.

36. The _____ region wanted high tariffs, no expansion of slavery and did not favor
    settling the west.

37. The most rural and agrarian of all regions in the United States in 1850 was the _____ .

38. Three of the original six states of the Confederacy were a. _____ ,
     b. _____ and c. _____ .

39. The Confederacy lost control of the Mississippi River and was cut in two when Grant captured
     _____ .

40. Because he opposed the harsh Reconstruction policies of the Republican radicals, President
     _____ was impeached but found not guilty.

70 / 87

Score
Teacher Check _____

Initial   Date

History & Geography 1106 Alternate Test

Name _____

Match these items (each answer, 2 points).

1.	_____ assembly line	a.	loyalty to one's country
2.	_____ Industrial Revolution	b.	attempt to halt European colonization in the Western Hemisphere
3.	_____ labor unions	c.	merging of capital by people who purchase a small part of a large business
4.	_____ imperialism	d.	Italy, Austria-Hungary, Germany
5.	_____ nationalism	e.	change from hand labor to machine production
6.	_____ urbanization	f.	organization of labor to improve workers' conditions
7.	_____ isolationism	g.	mass development of farm labor-saving equipment
8.	_____ Triple Alliance	h.	build-up of military forces
9.	_____ Monroe Doctrine	i.	colonization of smaller countries for raw materials
10.	_____ Big Stick Policy	j.	piece-assemblage of goods
11.	_____ corporations	k.	Roosevelt Corollary
12.	_____ Agricultural Revolution	l.	mass movement to the city
		m.	noninvolvement in world affairs.

Complete these statements (each answer, 3 points).

13. Eli Whitney's invention of the a. _____ and McCormick's invention of the b. _____ improved agriculture.

14. Two inventions that greatly improved transportation were Fulton's a. _____ and Cooper's b. _____ .

15. Morse's invention of the _____ aided communication and business transactions.

16. Telegraph transmissions between Britain and America were made possible by a (what?) _____ .

17. A new power source unleashed when Drake _____ .

18. The battle of San Juan was won by Roosevelt and his _____ .

19. Dewey's victory at Manila Bay brought American takeover of the _____ .

20. The "Iron Chancellor" who did much to secure Germany's defense was _____ .

21. The purchase of Alaska was sarcastically labeled _____ 's Folly.

22. Geothals was the brilliant builder of the _____ .

23. The Philippines, Guam and Puerto Rico became American possessions after the _____ .

Answer *true* or *false* (each answer, 1 point).

24. _____ As businesses grew, needing larger machinery and power sources, factories developed.

25. _____ The Clayton Anti-Trust Act and the Federal Trade Commission checked the growth of the labor movement.

26. _____ Rural folks were drawn by the higher wages and variety of life to the city.

27. _____ Labor unions not only represented the workers' plight to management, they also helped get many labor laws passed.

28. _____ A major problem in building the Panama Canal was disease.

29. _____ American trade with the Far East was improved by the policies of Hay and Perry.

30. _____ Prussia led Europe in military readiness techniques, such as conscription.

31. _____ Bismarck sought friends with Britain, France and Russia.

32. _____ European militarism showed itself in the build-up of arms, navies and fortifications of boundaries.

33. _____ The Triple Entente had control of the seas; the Alliance had strength in its unified location.

Write the correct letter for the answer on the line (each answer, 2 points).

34. Factors making America ripe for industry included all the following items *except* _____ .
    a. New England businessmen
    b. rivers to power industry
    c. determination to prove itself to Britain
    d. guidance from British industry

35. Factors encouraging American industrial growth included _____ .
    a. horses and mules
    b. modern machinery
    c. traditional production methods
    d. smaller market

61

36. Effects of corporations on American industry included _____ .
    a. monopolies on business
    b. higher prices
    c. use of fewer workers
    d. reduced production

37. The Spanish-American War resulted in _____ .
    a. Spanish possession of Guam and Puerto Rico
    b. American purchase of the Philippines
    c. American isolation
    d. Cuban colonization

38. One achievement that was not President Theodore Roosevelt's was_____ .
    a. American neutrality in the first years of World War I
    b. Japanese-Russian settlement
    c. enforcing of antitrust laws
    d. increasing American world involvement

39. The German action that brought European tension to the breaking point was _____ .
    a. German involvement in Australia
    b. the proposed German railroad
    c. the cutback of German navy
    d. Wilhelm's successful diplomacy

Answer these questions (each answer, 5 points).

40. How did nationalism and imperialism result in increased militarism in Europe?

    _____

    _____

    _____

    _____

41. In what ways was the average working man the victim of the Industrial Revolution?

    _____

    _____

    _____

    _____

76 / 95

Score
Teacher Check _____

Initial   Date

62

Name _____

Match these items (each answer, 2 points).

1. _____ Fourteen Points   a. sought to ban liquor sales

2. _____ Treaty of Versailles   b. mass movement to the cities

3. _____ League of Nations   c. renounced war as a way to settle disagreements

4. _____ urbanization   d. political and social reforms, began in 1880s

5. _____ prohibition   e. peace treaty following World War I

6. _____ progressivism   f. cut-back on federal spending

7. _____ disarmament   g. opposed movement for black rights

8. _____ isolationism   h. Wilson's organization for settling international differences

9. _____ internationalism   i. Wilson's plan for peace

10. _____ New Deal   j. involvement in world affairs

11. _____ Kellogg-Briand Pact   k. cut-back in military equipment

12. _____ Ku Klux Klan   l. Franklin D. Roosevelt's Depression recovery program

                                     m. noninvolvement in world affairs

Complete these statements (each answer, 3 points).

13. After World War I, President _____'s policies were rejected in favor of a more hedonistic way of life.

14. World War I was ignited by hostilities between _____ .

15. The amendment that created prohibition was the _____ Amendment.

16. One incident that led America into World War I was the sinking of the passenger ship _____ which killed 128 Americans.

17. Americans backed the return to normalcy policy of President _____ .

18. Much of the blame for the Great Depression was placed on _____ by the American people.

19. The Washington Disarmament Conference was concerned with limiting _____ .

20. Theodore Roosevelt and Woodrow Wilson greatly influenced the thinking of President _____ .

21. The American forces in World War I were commanded by _____ .

22. Britain, France and Russia were three members of the _____ in World War I.

Answer *true* or *false* (each answer, 1 point).

23. _____ Germany, Italy and Austria composed the Central Powers in World War I.

24. _____ World War I was triggered by the assassination of the president of Serbia.

25. _____ Most Allied nations supported Wilson's just peace at the Paris peace talks.

26. _____ America was weary of fighting causes and campaigns by 1919, thus rejecting Wilson's progressivism.

27. _____ Entertainment and better opportunities led many to the city.

28. _____ The prohibition movement was strongly backed by America's religious community.

29. _____ President Calvin Coolidge implemented programs of increased immigration.

30. _____ America, prosperous and productive in the '20s, was shocked by the fall of the stock market.

31. _____ The Great Depression left both executives and laborers unemployed and destitute.

32. _____ President Herbert Hoover placed too much hope in the private sector of American business to pull him out of the Depression.

Write the letter for the correct answer on the line (each answer, 2 points).

33. Events leading to the German surrender in World War I did not include _____ .
    a. collapse of German allies   c. Wilson's Fourteen Points
    b. American entry into the war   d. Berlin airlift

34. Programs supported during the Harding administration did not include _____ .
    a. TVA   c. Emergency Quota Act
    b. Tea Pot Dome Scandals   d. Immigration Act

35. One of the factors leading to the Great Depression was _____ .
    a. high employment rate   c. weak national economy
    b. credit balance   d. World War II

36. One piece of legislation combating the Great Depression was _____ .
    a. Fourteen Points   c. NATO
    b. Emergency Banking Act   d. League of Nations

37. The provisions of the Treaty of Versailles did *not* _____ .
    a. divide German possessions   c. follow Wilson's Fourteen Points
    b. end World War I   d. limit the German military

Answer these questions (each answer, 5 points).

38. How did America's entrance into 'World War I boost the Allied cause?

_____ .

_____ .

_____ .

_____ .

39. Why did the Great Depression take America by surprise?

_____ .

_____ .

_____ .

_____ .

| 67 / 84 |

Score
Teacher Check _____

Initial   Date

History & Geography 1108 Alternate Test

Name _____

Match these items (each answer, 2 points).

1. _____ Hitler

a. Cuban dictator following Cuban Revolution

2. _____ Eisenhower

b. the commander of Allied forces in Europe during World War II

3. _____ Churchill

c. president leading the United States into active military involvement in Vietnam

4. _____ Castro

d. the head of the People's Republic of China

5. _____ Khruschev

e. political advisor to Nixon on foreign affairs

6. _____ MacArthur

f. German Fuhrer during World War II

7. _____ Mussolini

g. president leading American withdrawal from Vietnam

8. _____ Johnson

h. commander of American forces in the Pacific during World War II

9. _____ Mao Zedong

i. the head of Chinese Nationalist Party

10. _____ Nixon

j. the head of the Communists' forces in Indo-China and Vietnam

11. _____ Ho Chi Minh

k. Italian dictator during World War II

12. _____ Kissinger

l. Soviet premier during Kennedy years

m. British prime minister during World War II

Complete these statements (each answer, 3 points).

13. The United States entered World War II when Japan attacked _____ .

14. The fighting in the Pacific in World War II ended with the bombing of a. _____ and b. _____ with atomic bombs.

15. In order to settle conflicts between nations in a peaceful way, the _____ was organized in 1945.

16. NATO and SEATO gave European and Asian nations a defense against _____ threat.

17. The Gulf of Tonkin resolution led to the in-depth military involvement by the United States in _____ .

18. President Nixon's plan to hand over the fighting to the South Vietnamese was called _____ .

19. The invasion of South Korea was stopped in 1950 at the _____ .

20. The nonshooting war between the United States and the Soviet Union was labeled the
_____ .

21. The Bay of Pigs and Cuban missile crisis were problems of the _____
administration.

22. The Axis powers of World War II were a. _____ , b. _____ ,
and c. _____ .

23. The three prominent Allied nations of World War II were a. _____ ,
b. _____ , and c. _____ .

Answer *true* or *false* (each answer, 1 point).

24. _____ The Allied victory of the battle of Normandy began the drive to take over France
and Germany.

25. _____ The United States and the Soviet Union sought no control over conquered nations
following World War II.

26. _____ The Marshall Plan offered financial aid to European nations threatened by
Communism.

27. _____ The United States victory at the Bay of Pigs checked Russian influence in Cuba.

28. _____ The fate of occupied nations of World War II rested on the Nuremberg meetings.

29. _____ At the height of his power, Hitler conquered France, Greece and Russia.

30. _____ MacArthur was forced to leave his command when he defied Truman's
containment policy in Korea.

31. _____ Doolittle's Raid on Tokyo gave the United States a much needed boost of morale
during the war in the Pacific.

32. _____ Ho Chi Minh opposed Ngo Dinh Deim in the Vietnamese civil war.

33. _____ Mao's People's Republic of China was formed after he drove the Chinese
Nationalists to Formosa.

Write the letter for the correct answer on the line (each answer, 2 points).

34. Allied victories in Europe during World War II did not include _____
   a. the Normandy invasion
   b. battle for Eastern Europe
   c. the drive through Italy
   d. Guadalcanal

35. United States efforts to check Communist expansion in Europe included _____
   a. ANZUS
   b. Marshall Plan
   c. Eisenhower Doctrine
   d. SEATO

36. American strategies in the Pacific in World War II included _____
   a. atomic bombing
   b. invasion of Japan itself
   c. propaganda
   d. economic pressure

37. The legal step leading the American military into Vietnam was _____
    a. Eisenhower's commitment to Ho Chi Minh
    b. Nixon's advisors
    c. Gulf of Tonkin resolution
    d. MacArthur's march to the border

38. Problems encountered in the United States as a result of the Vietnam involvement did *not* include _____
    a. drug use
    b. overcrowded armed forces
    c. distrust of government
    d. immorality

Answer this question (each answer, 5 points).

39. Why did the United Sates involve itself in other nations' civil wars as it did in Korea and Vietnam?

    _____

    _____

    _____

    _____

78 / 97

Score
Teacher Check _____

Initial   Date

Name _____

Answer *true* of *false* (each answer, 1 point).

1. _____ One of the most significant failures of the Johnson administration was the inability to solve the problem of Vietnam.

2. _____ President Johnson aggressively pursued the conflict in Vietnam after he was given broad powers with the passage of the Gulf of Tonkin resolution.

3. _____ President Johnson's election victory in 1964 allowed him to implement his New Frontier program.

4. _____ President Nixon began the policy of removing troops from Vietnam.

5. _____ One of Kennedy's outstanding contributions was the Nuclear Test Ban Treaty.

6. _____ President Nixon won respect for his domestic policies called New Internationalism.

7. _____ Detente opened the way for the SALT talks and reopening relations with China.

8. _____ One of the most significant changes of the 1970s took place as the Cold War policy of containment gave way to diplomacy of realism that led to detente.

9. _____ The Berlin Wall was built during the Johnson administration.

10. _____ Martin Luther King, Jr. was a civil rights leader of the 1960s.

Match these items (each answer, 2 points).

11. _____ Cuban Missile Crisis   a. Kennedy's program for America

12. _____ "sit-ins" at businesses   b. a Soviet astronaut

13. _____ John Glenn   c. crisis of Kennedy's presidency

14. _____ hawks   d. Communist guerrilla forces

15. _____ New Frontier   e. attempts to end racial segregation in the South

16. _____ cosmonaut   f. first American to orbit the earth

17. _____ Viet Cong   g. arms limitations agreements

18. _____ Neil Armstrong   h. those favoring the Vietnam war

19. _____ SALT   i. first American on the moon

20. _____ Henry Kissinger   j. Gerald Ford

                                      k. Nixon's secretary of state

Complete these statements (each answer, 3 points).

21. One of President Nixon's chief economic problems was _____ .

22. To attempt to remove a public official from office because of wrongdoing is called _____ .

23. An amnesty program for Vietnam war protesters was begun by _____ .

24. President Ford's foreign crisis as president was _____ .

25. President Ford's most controversial act was to _____ .

26. Those Americans who opposed the Vietnam War were called _____ .

27. President Nixon was the first president to visit communist _____ and _____ .

28. President Johnson was far more effective in domestic programs than was President _____ .

29. President Carter's great foreign policy triumph was the agreement between Egypt and Israel called the _____ .

30. Probably President Nixon's greatest failure as president was the _____ scandal.

Write the letter for the correct answer on the line (each answer, 2 points).

31. The president who did not run again because of Vietnam was _____ .
    a. Johnson   c. Ford
    b. Kennedy   d. Nixon

32. The Supreme Court tried to balance the races in all schools in a district by _____ .
    a. segregating   c. busing
    b negotiating   d. legislating

33. A sudden rise in prices that effects the cost of living is _____ .
    a. impeachment   c. deflation
    b. inflation   d. desegregation

34. One of the most imaginative, worthwhile and popular programs of the New Frontier was the _____ .
    a. freedom riders   c. economic policies
    b. space program   d. Peace Corps

35. The first SALT Treaty was signed under President _____ .
    a. Ford   c. Nixon
    b. Kennedy   d. Johnson

Score _____
Teacher Check _____

Initial   Date

Match these items (each answer, 2 points).

1. _____ astrolabe
2. _____ Atlantic triangle
3. _____ Freedman's Bureau
4. _____ colony at Jamestown
5. _____ Environmental Protection Agency
6. _____ South Carolina
7. _____ underground railroad
8. _____ League of Nations
9. _____ Watergate scandal
10. _____ Union blockade
11. _____ John Marshall
12. _____ Pearl Harbor
13. _____ Federal Trade Commission
14. _____ Crusades
15. _____ New Frontier

a. settled to give England raw materials
b. organization for world peace
c. tries to protect consumers rights
d. attempted to recapture Holy Land
e. Renaissance invention for guiding ships
f. Kennedy's program
g. Chief Justice of the Supreme Court
h. the slave-trading cycle
i. Nixon's answer to pollution crisis
j. founded to help former slaves after Civil War
k. network of escape routes for runaway slaves
l. Lyndon Johnson
m. first state to secede
n. attacked by Japan in 1941
o. successful Union strategy of the Civil War
p. forced Nixon to resign

Complete these statements (each answer, 3 points).

16. The Declaration of Independence was written by _____ .

17. Abraham Lincoln freed the slaves with the _____ Proclamation in 1862.

18. Alexander Graham Bell invented the _____ .

19. The Union general who accepted the surrender at Appomattox was _____ .

20. The military commander of the Southern army in the Civil War was _____ .

21. Franklin D. Roosevelt's program for action when he took office was called the _____ .

22. The Peace Corps was started by President _____ .

23. Johann Gutenberg invented the _____ .

24. One important shortcoming of the Articles of Confederation was that it did not provide for _____ .

25. The first step in Nixon's Vietnamization program was _____ .

Write the letter for the correct answer on the line (each answer, 2 points).

26. The civil rights legislation passed by Congress in 1964 was originated by President _____
    a. Kennedy
    b. Johnson
    c. Eisenhower
    d. Truman

27. The British right to enter an American home and confiscate goods during the Revolution came from a bill called a _____ .
    a. protective tariff
    b. Embargo Act
    c. Writ of Assistance
    d. Quartering policy

28. The war fought to determine which European nation controlled the North American continent was the _____
    a. American Revolution
    b. French and Indian War
    c. War of 1812
    d. crusades

29. After the Civil War the South was governed under the _____
    a. Civil Rights Act
    b. Freedman's Bureau
    c. Black Codes
    d. Reconstruction Act

30. The program established by Lyndon Johnson after his 1964 election was the _____ .
    a. Great Society
    b. New Deal
    c. New Frontier
    d. Imperialism

31. Abraham Lincoln was assassinated by _____ at Ford's Theater.
    a. Andrew Johnson
    b. John Wilkes Booth
    c. Samuel Morse
    d. Robert E. Lee

32. The first assembly line was set up by _____ .
    a. John Smith
    b. Herbert Hoover
    c. Eli Whitney
    d. Henry Ford

33. Controversy between the Virginia Plan and the New Jersey Plan of congressional representation was settled by the _____ .
    a. Great Compromise
    b. New Internationalism
    c. Reconstruction Act
    d. Trade Rights Bill

34. The Supreme Court first declared an act of Congress unconstitutional in the _____ decision.
    a. *Brown vs. Board of Education*
    b. Civil Rights Act
    c. *Marbury vs. Madison*
    d. Voting Rights

35. The man who succeeded Nixon as president was President _____ .
    a. Rockefeller
    b. Ford
    c. Carter
    d. Johnson

Answer *true* or *false* (each answer, 1 point).

36. _____ The Great Depression began when Hoover was president.

37. _____ Adolf Hitler was the dictator of Italy in World War I.

38. _____ John Smith led the English colony at Jamestown.

39. _____ Andrew Johnson took over the presidency when Lincoln was killed.

40. _____ The treaty ending World War I was signed at Appomattox.

Score
Teacher Check _____

Initial   **Date**

ANSWER KEYS

SECTION 1

1.1	e
1.2	a
1.3	b
1.4	d
1.5	c
1.6	c
1.7	b
1.8	d
1.9	Crusades
1.10	Arabia
1.11	North Africa; Spain
1.12	Roman Catholic
1.13	Saracens
1.14	200
1.15	trade
1.16	bourgeoisie
1.17	gold and silver
1.18	c
1.19	b
1.20	f
1.21	a
1.22	d
1.23	e
1.24	true
1.25	false
1.26	Latin
1.27	c
1.28	b
1.29	a
1.30	d
1.31	a
1.32	b
1.33	d
1.34	a
1.35	trade
1.36	colonies; import
1.37	Martin Luther and John Calvin
1.38	true

SECTION 2

2.1	m
2.2	k
2.3	l
2.4	e
2.5	c
2.6	i
2.7	d
2.8	j
2.9	b
2.10	h
2.11	a
2.12	g
2.13	f
2.14	capital
2.15	Richard Hakluyt
2.16	joint-stock
2.17	d
2.18	a
2.19	f
2.20	b
2.21	c
2.22	e
2.23	Jamestown started with men seeking fortunes and greater measures of liberty and adventure in the New World.
2.24	b, c
2.25	gentlemen; skilled craftsmen; farmers; doctors
2.26	John Smith
2.27	John Rolfe
2.28	London; Northwest
2.29	burgesses
2.30	tidewater; piedmont
2.31	indentured servant
2.32	tidewater; piedmont
2.33	House of Burgesses
2.34	Pocahontas
2.35	Nathaniel Bacon
2.36	a, b, d
2.37	c
2.38	e
2.39	b
2.40	a
2.41	d
2.42	False
2.43	False
2.44	False
2.45	False
2.46	False
2.47	False
2.48	d
2.49	c
2.50	b
2.51	a
2.52	True
2.53	True
2.54	False
2.55	supplies; London Company
2.56	Mayflower Compact
2.57	John Carver; William Bradford
2.58	Samoset; Squanto
2.59	fort; church; homes
2.60	two months

2.61	True	3.14	New York
2.62	True	3.15	New Jersey
2.63	True	3.16	True
2.64	False	3.17	False
2.65	True	3.18	False
2.66	True	3.19	government; universities; military service
2.67	True	3.20	John Berkeley
2.68	False	3.21	East Jersey; West Jersey
2.69	False	3.22	Pennsylvania
2.70	True	3.23	Society of Friends
2.71	False	3.24	William Penn
2.72	False	3.25	Philadelphia; City of Brotherly Love
2.73	True	3.26	Germans/pennsylvania Dutch; Scotch-Irish
2.74	religious	3.27	Swedes; Dutch
2.75	Newport	3.28	coastline
2.76	Jews; Quakers; Separatists	3.29	False
2.77	paid	3.30	True
2.78	Thomas Hooker	3.31	False
2.79	Government; land	3.32	True
2.80	Hartford; Wethersfield; Windsor	3.33	Virginia; (Spanish) Florida
2.81	Gorges; Mason	3.34	Virginia
2.82	Massachusetts Bay Colony	3.35	Charleston
2.83	1679	3.36	royal
2.84	1820	3.37	Georgia
2.85	He was not sympathetic to the Puritan colonists. He ruled harshly and imposed heavy taxes. He wanted the Puritans to open their meeting houses for Church of England services.	3.38	James Oglethorpe
		3.39	b, d, g, h
		3.40	a, c, e, f
		3.41	To have a colony south of the Carolinas that would serve as a buffer to keep the Spanish from moving further northward; to provide a home and a new life for British prisoners and convicts.
2.86	e		
2.87	d		
2.88	f		
2.89	c	3.42	families; immigration
2.90	g	3.43	farming; fishing, lumbering, fur trading, commerce business
2.91	b		
2.92	h	3.44	colonial merchants
2.93	a	3.45	Germans; Scotch-Irish; (French) Huguenots

Section 3

		3.46	Africa
3.1	a	3.47	communication; transportation
3.2	d	3.48	a, b, c
3.3	b	3.49	d, e
3.4	c	3.50	c
3.5	proprietary	3.51	b
3.6	Maryland	3.52	c
3.7	Catholics; Lord Baltimore	3.53	b
3.8	Toleration	3.54	False
3.9	Manhattan; 24	3.55	True
3.10	illegal trade		
3.11	fur trade		
3.12	Peter Stuyvesant		
3.13	1664		

SECTION 1

1.1	d
1.2	a
1.3	b
1.4	c
1.5	f
1.6	e
1.7	false
1.8	true
1.9	mercantile
1.10	James Otis
1.11	tobacco, sugar, indigo, naval stores, molasses, furs
1.12	Molasses Act of 1733 Wool Act of 1699 Sugar Act of 1764 Hat Act of 1732
1.13	America sent raw materials to England and had to buy manufactured goods back. Raw material costs less than manufactured goods; therefore, England made more money.
1.14	b
1.15	d
1.16	c
1.17	b
1.18	b
1.19	d
1.20	b
1.21	c
1.22	furs (animals\beavers) Indians (Natives)
1.23	Iroquois
1.24	Duquesne
1.25	boycott
1.26	b
1.27	a
1.28	e
1.29	d
1.30	c
1.31	g
1.32	f
1.33	b
1.34	c
1.35	a
1.36	d
1.37	c

SECTION 2

2.1	compromise
2.2	cannons
2.3	George Washington
2.4	Olive Branch Petition
2.5	mercenaries
2.6	Hessians
2.7	Gage
2.8	Fort Ticonderoga
2.9	Benedict Arnold; Montgomery
2.10	Common Sense; Great Britain
2.11	Richard Henry Lee
2.12	Thomas Jefferson
2.13	taxes
2.14	gold; silver
2.15	a
2.16	b, c, d
2.17	c
2.18	b
2.19	a
2.20	Trenton Bunker Hill New York Princeton Saratoga Philadelphia
2.21	British
2.22	Loyalist
2.23	British
2.24	Washington
2.25	Trenton
2.26	The courage of the Continental Soldiers, the leadership of George Washington and help from foreign countries
2.27	Inspector General
2.28	true
2.29	false
2.30	a, d, e, g
2.31	false
2.32	false
2.33	true
2.34	false
2.35	true
2.36	true
2.37	Nathaniel Greene
2.38	Illinois and Indiana
2.39	"Great Lakes"; Ohio River and the Mississippi River
2.40	forty
2.41	yet begun to fight
2.42	privateer
2.43	John Paul Jones
2.44	West Point
2.45	Saratoga
2.46	that I have but one life to lose for my country
2.47	Virginia

2.48   c
2.49   a
2.50   b
2.51   e
2.52   d
2.53   b

Section 3

3.1   democracy
3.2   emancipation
3.3   Spain
3.4   100,000
3.5   19,000; 4,000
3.6   December 4, 1783
3.7   Fraunces Tavern
3.8   Vermont
3.9   Separation; state
3.10   Rhode Island
3.11   Pennsylvania and Massachusetts
3.12   George Washington
3.13   public
3.14   d
3.15   b
3.16   c
3.17   c
3.18   b
3.19   b
3.20   c
3.21   b
3.22   a
3.23   d
3.24   60,000
3.25   So the delegates could feel free to change
        their minds as new information was
        presented.
3.26   b, d and f
3.27   b, c and e
3.28   Federalists; Antifederalists
3.29   a
3.30   Virginia; New Jersey

SECTION 1

1.1	d
1.2	e
1.3	a
1.4	b
1.5	c
1.6	f
1.7	c
1.8	g
1.9	a
1.10	b
1.11	h
1.12	d
1.13	f
1.14	e
1.15	a
1.16	c
1.17	c
1.18	a, c, e, g
1.19	b
1.20	a, b, d
1.21	True
1.22	George Washington
1.23	Constitution
1.24	caucus
1.25	Federalist; Democratic-Republican
1.26	impress
1.27	neutrality
1.28	shipping
1.29	West Florida
1.30	alliances
1.31	capture
1.32	money
1.33	Kentucky and Virginia
1.34	Federalist
1.35	Twelfth
1.36	false
1.37	true
1.38	false
1.39	true
1.40	c
1.41	d
1.42	f
1.43	e
1.44	b
1.45	a
1.46	b

SECTION 2

2.1	b
2.2	b
2.3	d
2.4	c
2.5	b
2.6	b
2.7	d
2.8	James Monroe
2.9	James Monroe; Robert Livingston
2.10	true
2.11	false
2.12	true
2.13	false
2.14	true
2.15	c
2.16	c
2.17	true
2.18	true
2.19	false
2.20	false
2.21	false
2.22	false
2.23	false
2.24	true
2.25	e
2.26	a
2.27	c
2.28	b
2.29	d
2.30	15
2.31	McHenry
2.32	(1) America gained the respect of foreign nations by proving to the world that it could take a stand against Britain. (2) When imported manufactured goods were no longer available because of the British blockade of American ships, American industry was forced to produce its own products. (3) Americans were proud of their efforts during the war and a new spirit of nationalism was created. (4) America was now ready to expand westward because the Indians had been crushed and the British had abandoned their forts.
2.33	All boundaries were restored to their pre-war locations and the two nations agreed to stop fighting.

Section 3

3.1	Monroe Doctrine
3.2	Supreme Court
3.3	British
3.4	bankruptcy
3.5	federal government; Supreme Court
3.6	treaty

3.7   unimportant

3.8   turnpikes

3.9   8; 90%

3.10   The United States would not take part in any foreign wars. The United States would not interfere with any existing European colonies. The American continents were not subject to future colonization by European powers. Any attempt by European powers to further colonize the United States would be considered a threat to America's peace and safety.

3.11   b, c

3.12   a

3.13   c

3.14   e

3.15   b

3.16   d

3.17   g

3.18   f

3.19   b

3.20   e

3.21   c

3.22   a

3.23   d

3.24   f

3.25   a, e

3.26   c, d

3.27   b, f

3.28   True

3.29   True

3.30   False

3.31   True

3.32   False

3.33   False

3.34   True

3.35   sectional

3.36   John Quincy Adams; William H. Crawford; Henry Clay; Andrew Jackson

3.37   National Republicans; Democrats

3.38   monster

3.39   a

3.40   a

3.41   c

3.42   d

3.43   c

3.44   b

3.45   West

3.46   against

SECTION 1

1.1	i
1.2	k
1.3	b
1.4	j
1.5	c
1.6	e
1.7	a
1.8	f
1.9	h
1.10	d
1.11	l
1.12	g
1.13	false
1.14	slave owners
1.15	Embargo
1.16	nullification
1.17	compromise
1.18	buttress
1.19	reduced
1.20	25
1.21	a
1.22	a, b, d, f
1.23	a, c, f
1.24	d
1.25	false
1.26	true
1.27	true
1.28	false
1.29	c
1.30	c
1.31	c
1.32	b
1.33	b
1.34	b, d
1.35	c
1.36	b
1.37	San Francisco; San Diego
1.38	Texas; state
1.39	Sutter's; Sacramento
1.40	Mexico City
1.41	b
1.42	d
1.43	a
1.44	b
1.45	a
1.46	a
1.47	b
1.48	Chicago; St. Louise; Memphis; New Orleans
1.49	1,000; 6,000
1.50	Bleeding Kansas
1.51	Immigrant Society
1.52	Sumner; Kansas
1.53	c
1.54	d
1.55	a
1.56	b
1.57	f
1.58	e
1.59	fugitive slave
1.60	personal liberty
1.61	Freeport Doctrine
1.62	little Eva; Uncle Tom; Simon Legree
1.63	abolitionist
1.64	Harper's Ferry; Virginia
1.65	Robert E. Lee; J.E.B. Stuart
1.66	hanged
1.67	false
1.68	true
1.69	Example: Douglas advocated popular sovereignty in a series of debates with Abraham Lincoln. He explained that slavery could only exist if the state legislature passed laws protecting slave property and could, therefore, curtail slavery without banning it outright.
1.70	Example: Lincoln claimed that a divided nation could not stand. His view was that the nation would eventually be either completely free or completely slave. However, people in the North and South thought he was advocating war. He did not imply interference with the status of slavery but opposed the extension of slavery.

SECTION 2

2.1	Civil War
2.2	field workers; house slaves; skilled craftsmen
2.3	tobacco; sugar; hemp; cotton
2.4	Eli Whitney
2.5	Louisiana
2.6	Kentucky; Maryland; Delaware; Virginia
2.7	working
2.8	whipping
2.9	to be free
2.10	Liberia
2.11	Sierra Leone
2.12	d
2.13	a
2.14	e
2.15	b
2.16	f
2.17	c

2.18   b, d, e
2.19   a, b, f
2.20   a, b, e, f, h
2.21   c
2.22   a
2.23   e
2.24   h
2.25   b
2.26   j
2.27   d
2.28   f
2.29   g
2.30   i
2.31   b, e, f, g, h, i
2.32   c
2.33   d
2.34   b
2.35   "The Farewell;" Uncle Tom's Cabin
2.36   true
2.37   true
2.38   false
2.39   true
2.40   true
2.41   b
2.42   d
2.43   e
2.44   c
2.45   a

SECTION 1

1.1 New York; 3,048,325
1.2 Rhode Island; 143,875
1.3 Massachusetts; 127.5
1.4 Connecticut
1.5 ten
1.6 d
1.7 g
1.8 e
1.9 b
1.10 f
1.11 a
1.12 c

1.13

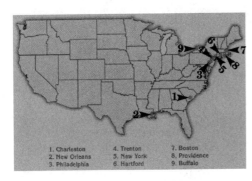

1. Charleston   4. Trenton   7. Boston
2. New Orleans   5. New York   8. Providence
3. Philadelphia 6. Hartford   9. Buffalo

1.14 c, e
1.15 d
1.16 c
1.17 e
1.18 a
1.19 b
1.20 b
1.21 a
1.22 d
1.23 b
1.24 a
1.25 c
1.26 a
1.27 Missouri, Arkansas, Tennessee, Kentucky
1.28 6,948,426
1.29 Ohio, 1,955,050
1.30 Ohio
1.31 Tennessee
1.32 Minnesota
1.33 true
1.34 false
1.35 true
1.36 true

1.37

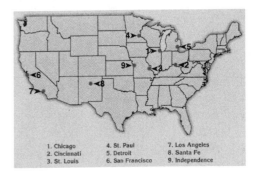

1. Chicago   4. St. Paul   7. Los Angeles
2. Cincinnati   5. Detroit   8. Santa Fe
3. St. Louis   6. San Francisco 9. Independence

1.38 b
1.39 c
1.40 a
1.41 d
1.42 2,576,090
1.43 584,962
1.44 3,161,052
1.45 Virginia
1.46 Texas; Maryland
1.47 Delaware
1.48 agriculture
1.49 cotton, tobacco, rice, sugar, hemp, indigo
1.50 Maryland, Delaware, Virginia, North Carolina, South Carolina, Georgia

1.51

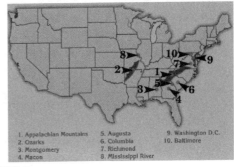

1. Appalachian Mountains   5. Augusta   9. Washington D.C.
2. Ozarks   6. Columbia   10. Baltimore
3. Montgomery   7. Richmond
4. Macon   8. Mississippi River

SECTION 2

2.1 specie
2.2 Republican
2.3 John Breckenridge
2.4 Stephen Douglas
2.5 Jefferson Davis
2.6 Alexander Stephens
2.7 North Carolina, Tennessee, Arkansas, Virginia
2.8 Robert E. Lee
2.9 to use force
2.10 false
2.11 true
2.12 false
2.13 true
2.14 true
2.15 true
2.16 true
2.17 true
2.18 false

2.19	true		2.71	false
2.20	b		2.72	false
2.21	a, d, e		2.73	Vicksburg
2.22	d		2.74	July 4, 1863
2.23	b, d, f, g, j, k		2.75	supplies; communications
2.24	north		2.76	south
2.25	north		2.77	Chattanooga; Grant; Sherman
2.26	south		2.78	55,000
2.27	north		2.79	Petersburg; nine
2.28	south		2.80	General George McClellan
2.29	south		2.81	Andrew Johnson
2.30	north		2.82	212; 55
2.31	south		2.83	60; 300
2.32	north		2.84	Hampton Roads; Appomattox
2.33	north		2.85	
2.34	a, d, e			
2.35	West Point			
2.36	cotton, Britain, France			
2.37	Richmond, Virginia			
2.38	c			
2.39	d			
2.40	a			
2.41	e			
2.42	b			
2.43	264; 300			
2.44	Robert Smalls			
2.45	Monitor; Merrimac			
2.46	it was the first battle of metal plated ships			
2.47	divide and conquer			
2.48	Robert E. Lee			
2.49	Captain David Farragut; Benjamin R. Butler			

Important Civil War Sites

1. Appomattox
2. Atlanta, GA
3. Bull Run
4. Chattanooga, TN
5. Fort Donelson
6. Fort Sumter
7. Gettysburg
8. Hampton Roads
9. Harper's Ferry
10. Montgomery, AL
11. Port Hudson, LA
12. Potomac River
13. Savannah, GA
14. Vicksburg, MS

2.50	b		**Section 3**	
2.51	g		3.1	d
2.52	e		3.2	e
2.53	f		3.3	c
2.54	a		3.4	a
2.55	c		3.5	f
2.56	d		3.6	b
2.57	b		3.7	b
2.58	c		3.8	g
2.59	a		3.9	a
2.60	a		3.10	e
2.61	d		3.11	c
2.62	c		3.12	d
2.63	true		3.13	f
2.64	true		3.14	a, c, e, h, i
2.65	false		3.15	b, c, g, i
2.66	true		3.16	a
2.67	false		3.17	d
2.68	false		3.18	b
2.69	true		3.19	c
2.70	true		3.20	a
			3.21	b
			3.22	Ku Klux Klan; Knights of the White Camelia; White Brotherhood
			3.23	Force Act
			3.24	Amnesty Act
			3.25	poll tax; literacy test
			3.26	Samuel Tilden; Rutherford B. Hayes

SECTION 1

1.1	a, b, d
1.2	a, b, d, e
1.3	a, c, d
1.4	a, b, c, d
1.5	isolationism
1.6	monopoly
1.7	costs
1.8	e
1.9	c
1.10	b
1.11	a
1.12	g
1.13	d
1.14	h
1.15	f
1.16	false
1.17	true
1.18	true
1.19	true
1.20	false
1.21	false
1.22	internal combustion
1.23	standardized parts
1.24	steam engine
1.25	Francis C. Lowell
1.26	Eli Whitney
1.27	Henry Ford
1.28	Middle Atlantic, North Central
1.29	capital
1.30	food products, textiles, iron and steel, lumber/forestry
1.31	large, expensive; power,
1.32	b
1.33	c
1.34	d
1.35	a
1.36	e
1.37	a
1.38	d
1.39	c
1.40	f
1.41	g
1.42	b
1.43	a, b, d, e
1.44	a, c, d
1.45	a, b, c, f

SECTION 2

2.1	c
2.2	a
2.3	b
2.4	b
2.5	e
2.6	a
2.7	c
2.8	d
2.9	a, b, c, d
2.10	a, c, d, e
2.11	a, b, d, e, f
2.12	a, b, c
2.13	a, b, c, d
2.14	factory; farm
2.15	tenements; fresh air
2.16	unhealthy; satisfactory
2.17	everybody worked; healthy, wholesome
2.18	little time for; quiet life
2.19	poor; pride in work
2.20	insignificant; good
2.21	crime, long hours; fewer difficulties
2.22	true
2.23	false
2.24	false
2.25	true
2.26	managers & workers
2.27	wages
2.28	layoff
2.29	unemployment insurance
2.30	unite
2.31	National Labor Union
2.32	monopolies
2.33	Uriah S. Stephens
2.34	Samuel Gompers
2.35	true
2.36	false
2.37	true
2.38	true
2.39	false
2.40	true
2.41	true
2.42	They had once managed a business and were proud of their skills; now they were working for another and paid the same as an unskilled man. They lost pride in their skills.
2.43	a, b, d, e
2.44	a, b, c
2.45	a, c, d, e
2.46	d
2.47	a
2.48	b
2.49	c

Section 3

3.1	isolationism
3.2	protectorate

History & Geography 1106 Answer Key

3.3   Monroe Doctrine
3.4   Russia; 1867; Seward's Folly or Icebox
3.5   William Seward
3.6   raw
3.7   North America; South America
3.8   defense; raw materials (resources)
3.9   Cuban, Spain
3.10   immigrants; newspapers
3.11   Spanish Ambassador; explosion
3.12   independence; ownership/control
3.13   true
3.14   true
3.15   Manila Bay–naval–Spanish; Manila
3.16   Santiago–naval–destroyed
3.17   San Juan Hill–land–United States
3.18   Puerto Rico–land–Puerto Rico
3.19   corollary
3.20   invasion
3.21   b
3.22   a
3.23   f
3.24   c
3.25   e
3.26   d
3.27   false
3.28   true
3.29   false
3.30   true
3.31   true
3.32   false
3.33   true
3.34   e
3.35   h
3.36   b
3.37   a
3.38   c
3.39   g
3.40   d
3.41   i
3.42   f
3.43   a, b, d, e
3.44   a, b, c
3.45   a, c, d
3.46   a, b, d, e
3.47   a, b, d
3.48   b
3.49   b, d
3.50   a, b
3.51   a, b, c, e

SECTION 4
4.1   c
4.2   a

4.3   b
4.4   militarism
4.5   Prussia
4.6   conscription
4.7   Chancellor
4.8   entente
4.9   true
4.10   true
4.11   true
4.12   false
4.13   false
4.14   false
4.15   false
4.16   true
4.17   false
4.18   true
4.19   true
4.20   false
4.21   false
4.22   false
4.23   a, b, c, e
4.24   a, c, d, e
4.25   a, b, d, e
4.26   b, c
4.27   b
4.28   d
4.29   e
4.30   b
4.31   c
4.32   a
4.33   b
4.34   a
4.35   e
4.36   c
4.37   d
4.38   Example: Loyalty to one's country is a desirable characteristic, raising the spirits of a country, especially in time of war and giving birth to pride in one's heritage. When nationalism goes to extremes, though, interfering with negotiations and cooperation, it becomes a disadvantage giving rise to conflict.

SECTION 1

1.1	a, b, c, e
1.2	a, d, e
1.3	a, b, d, e
1.4	a, b, c
1.5	a, c, d
1.6	a, b, c, e
1.7	a, b, d, e, f
1.8	armistice
1.9	stalemate
1.10	false
1.11	true
1.12	true
1.13	false
1.14	false
1.15	false
1.16	true
1.17	false
1.18	true
1.19	false
1.20	The continued loss of American lives due to the sinking of trading vessels by the German submarine blockade of Europe forced the United States into the conflict.
1.21	false
1.22	true
1.23	true
1.24	false
1.25	false
1.26	a, d, e
1.27	b, c, f
1.28	c
1.29	f
1.30	b
1.31	a
1.32	g
1.33	e
1.34	d
1.35	vengeance
1.36	reparations
1.37	b
1.38	e
1.39	a
1.40	e
1.41	a

SECTION 2

2.1	e
2.2	a
2.3	d
2.4	c
2.5	g
2.6	b
2.7	f
2.8	f
2.9	a
2.10	e
2.11	b
2.12	d
2.13	c
2.14	false
2.15	true
2.16	false
2.17	true
2.18	true
2.19	true
2.20	false
2.21	true
2.22	true
2.23	true
2.24	true
2.25	false
2.26	false
2.27	true
2.28	a
2.29	c
2.30	b
2.31	e
2.32	d
2.33	f
2.34	a, b
2.35	Advantages–consumption of alcohol decreased, along with a decrease in alcoholism and related diseases. Disadvantages–organized crime thrived on illegal liquor, thus gangs and their crimes increased.

Section 3

3.1	b
3.2	c
3.3	a
3.4	i
3.5	d
3.6	e
3.7	j
3.8	a
3.9	f
3.10	h
3.11	b
3.12	g
3.13	c
3.14	Stanford
3.15	secretary of commerce

3.16 "Greater Seminole," "Oklahoma City"
3.17 American Federation of Labor
3.18 true
3.19 false
3.20 true
3.21 false
3.22 a, c, d
3.23 b, d, e
3.24 c
3.25 a
3.26 d
3.27 b
3.28 e
3.29 Such large profits had been made prior to 1929 that the Depression cutback only curtailed large increases in profits.
3.30 He approved a loan from the Reconstruction Finance corporation for direct relief and created the Home Loan Bank System to aid homeowners about to lose their homes.

Section 4
4.1 true
4.2 true
4.3 true
4.4 true
4.5 true
4.6 false
4.7 true
4.8 false
4.9 false
4.10 true
4.11 b, c, e, f, g, j
4.12 b
4.13 a
4.14 d
4.15 c
4.16 e
4.17 FDR's background for president included experience in state and federal positions. As governor of New York he had organized a large relief effort there when the Depression began. He had battled back from polio and knew how to fight for what he wanted.
4.18 New York
4.19 1932
4.20 polio
4.21 Woodrow Wilson, Theodore Roosevelt
4.22 government
4.23 bottom up

4.24 "The only thing we have to fear is fear itself."
4.25 c
4.26 b
4.27 a

SECTION 1

1.1	g
1.2	c
1.3	b
1.4	e
1.5	a
1.6	d
1.7	f
1.8	true
1.9	false
1.10	false
1.11	true
1.12	false
1.13	true
1.14	false
1.15	true
1.16	military
1.17	Versailles
1.18	a, d, e, f
1.19	b
1.20	a, d
1.21	a, b, d
1.22	a
1.23	d
1.24	a
1.25	They used force to take what they wanted and their desire for power increased.
1.26	c
1.27	b
1.28	a
1.29	The Allies drove the Germans and Italians from North Africa; then they swept through Italy, overpowering them; next the Normandy invasion began a successful drive across France into Germany with the Soviets closing in from the east and Allies of the west.
1.30	The poor weather made the pinpointing of drop zones for paratroopers difficult–many missed their targets. Also, glider target areas were misjudged and many gliders crashed, killing their pilots. The conditions hurt the Allied forces, but at least confusion was cause for the Germans.
1.31	a
1.32	b
1.33	c
1.34	a, c
1.35	a, c, d
1.36	a, b, d
1.37	a, b
1.38	c
1.39	e
1.40	f

1.41	b
1.42	d
1.43	a
1.44	true
1.45	false
1.46	true
1.47	false
1.48	true
1.49	true
1.50	false
1.51	true
1.52	false
1.53	true

SECTION 2

2.1	Ratified
2.2	true
2.3	false
2.4	false
2.5	true
2.6	false
2.7	true
2.8	false
2.9	c
2.10	a
2.11	b
2.12	a, b, c, e
2.13	a
2.14	c
2.15	b
2.16	a
2.17	f
2.18	d
2.19	c
2.20	e
2.21	a, c, d, e
2.22	b
2.23	a
2.24	false
2.25	true
2.26	true
2.27	false
2.28	false
2.29	true
2.30	h
2.31	a
2.32	c
2.33	b
2.34	e
2.35	f
2.36	d
2.37	g
2.38	a

2.39   d
2.40   e
2.41   f
2.42   c
2.43   b

Section 3
3.1   b
3.2   d
3.3   c
3.4   a
3.5   a
3.6   c
3.7   e
3.8   b
3.9   d
3.10   true
3.11   false
3.12   false
3.13   true
3.14   true
3.15   false
3.16   They reached out to underdeveloped nations, sharing the wealth, knowledge and concern of people in the United States to improve lifestyles around the world.
3.17   a, b, d
3.18   a, b, c
3.19   a, b, d
3.20   d
3.21   a
3.22   b
3.23   e
3.24   c
3.25   Communist, Asia
3.26   Romans 13:17 sets the Christian standard for obedience to the government whose power is ordained by God, therefore, the Christian should back his government, then use his right to vote or voice his opinion to change policies when proper to do so.
3.27   true
3.28   true
3.29   false
3.30   true
3.31   pacifist
3.32   not to run
3.33   Vietnamization
3.34   Henry Kissinger
3.35   Paris
3.36   a, b
3.37   a, b, d

SECTION 1

1.1	f
1.2	a
1.3	e
1.4	b
1.5	d
1.6	c
1.7	Vietnam
1.8	Camelot
1.9	New Frontier
1.10	1960s
1.11	non-violent
1.12	true
1.13	false
1.14	false
1.15	true
1.16	true
1.17	true
1.18	b
1.19	c
1.20	g
1.21	b
1.22	a
1.23	f
1.24	d
1.25	e
1.26	h
1.27	true
1.28	true
1.29	true
1.30	false
1.31	true
1.32	false
1.33	false
1.34	true
1.35	true
1.36	true
1.37	a, d
1.38	c
1.39	d
1.40	a, d, e
1.41	d
1.42	draft or Vietnam War
1.43	Cuba
1.44	1961, 1989
1.45	quarantine or blockade
1.46	1999

SECTION 2

2.1	b
2.2	d
2.3	a
2.4	c
2.5	f
2.6	e
2.7	1968
2.8	Apollo
2.9	Vietnamization
2.10	Kent State University
2.11	eighteen
2.12	d
2.13	a, c, d, f
2.14	true
2.15	cruise missile
2.16	Gerald Ford
2.17	pardoned
2.18	*Roe v. Wade*
2.19	*Mayaguez*
2.20	Egypt, Israel
2.21	Iran
2.22	Afghanistan
2.23	b, d, e
2.24	false
2.25	true
2.26	true
2.27	false
2.28	false
2.29	true
2.30	true
2.31	c
2.32	a
2.33	b
2.34	d

Section 3

3.1	b
3.2	c
3.3	a
3.4	Star Wars
3.5	actor
3.6	1980
3.7	Communicator
3.8	Reaganomics
3.9	Sandra Day O'Conner
3.10	Geraldine Ferraro
3.11	Columbia
3.12	Bill Clinton
3.13	Right to Life, Operation Rescue, Crisis Pregnancy Center
3.14	b
3.15	d
3.16	c
3.17	a
3.18	true
3.19	true
3.20	true

3.21   true
3.22   true
3.23   true
3.24   c
3.25   a
3.26   b
3.27   e
3.28   c
3.29   i
3.30   f
3.31   a
3.32   b
3.33   d
3.34   h
3.35   g
3.36   b
3.37   d
3.38   a
3.39   c
3.40   true
3.41   false
3.42   true
3.43   NAFTA
3.44   Goals 2000
3.45   Acquired Immune Deficiency Syndrome

Section 4
4.1   false
4.2   true
4.3   false
4.4   false
4.5   false
4.6   false
4.7   true
4.8   true
4.9   c. Kenya
4.10   a. the 9-11 terrorist attacks
4.11   b. Hillary Clinton
4.12   d. Texas
4.13   d. United States Supreme Court
4.14   false
4.15   true
4.16   false
4.17   true
4.18   true
4.19   c. Indian
4.20   b. Pentagon
4.21   b. in a hole
4.22   b. 1/3
4.23   c. Afganistan

SECTION 1

1.1   c
1.2   d
1.3   b
1.4   e
1.5   a
1.6   Any order:
      noblemen
      serfs
      clergy
1.7   noblemen
1.8   jealousies and mistrust between noblemen
1.9   clergy
1.10   Muslims
1.11   The Crusades caused the armies of people to see that people in the East had luxuries that they did not have. Trade between Europeans and Italian merchants caused serfs to leave their villages for a better way of life. Producers of goods challenged the noblemen's right to own land. The power and wealth of the noblemen subsequently broke down.
1.12   a richer way of life
1.13   Any order:
      printing press
      education for reading and writing
      scientific progress
1.14   learning
1.15   printing press
1.16   Either order:
      raw materials (resources)
      food
1.17   mercantilism
1.18   discovery
1.19   finance
1.20   Any three: Africa, India, the Far East or the New World
1.21   e
1.22   i
1.23   g
1.24   h
1.25   a
1.26   b
1.27   c
1.28   j
1.29   f
1.30   d
1.31   Example: political struggles leading to self-government, fear of the Spanish.
1.32   Richard Hakluyt
1.33   Roanoke (Island)
1.34   no one knows

1.35   people could watch for approaching ships because it afforded protection from the Indians
1.36   John Smith
1.37   Any order:
      Governor
      Council
      Elected representatives from settlements
1.38   7.   Fundamental Orders of Connecticut
      5.   Massachusetts becomes a royal colony
      6.   Providence Plantations is founded
      2.   Puritans travel to Holland
      3.   Pilgrims set sail on the Mayflower
      1.   The Protestant Reformation
      4.   Puritans settle Massachusetts
1.39   religious freedom
1.40   John Calvin
1.41   Separatists
1.42   Mayflower Compact
1.43   Either order:
      He spoke out against religious laws made by the government.
      He believed Indians should be paid for land taken over by colonist.
1.44   Fundamental Orders of Connecticut
1.45   d
1.46   f
1.47   e
1.48   a
1.49   g
1.50   b
1.51   c
1.52   b
1.53   d
1.54   e
1.55   f
1.56   c
1.57   a

SECTION 2

2.1   b
2.2   d
2.3   a
2.4   c
2.5   Any three of the following:
      Molasses Act
      Wool Act
      Iron Act,
      Hat Act,
      Sugar Act
2.6   French and Indian War
2.7   eastern coast
2.8   independence; military

2.9   c

2.10   e

2.11   g

2.12   a

2.13   f

2.14   d

2.15   b

2.16   September 1774

2.17   the Intolerable Acts

2.18   meet again if grievances against Britain were not settled

2.19   life, liberty, property, taxation control

2.20   war

2.21   Lafayette

2.22   c

2.23   a

2.24   b

2.25   Example:
Explain to the king and Parliament the reasons the colonists were fighting the British in Boston.

2.26   Example:
It was the only way for the colonists to prevent Britain from exercising power over them.

2.27   Any order:
rights
government

2.28   b

2.29   d

2.30   f

2.31   e

2.32   c

2.33   a

2.34   c

2.35   e

2.36   b

2.37   d

2.38   a

2.39   balk

2.40   immune

2.41   Any order:
a. equal voting powers causing disputes between large and small states
b. Congress had power to levy taxes but no power to collect taxes
c. lacked strong powers
d. Congress could not control trade or commerce

2.42   George Washington

2.43   according to the free population of each state

2.44   judicial, legislative, executive

2.45   the New Jersey Plan

2.46   a House membership based on population and a Senate with equal representation

2.47   it divides power between the federal government and the stated and local governments

2.48   c

2.49   a

2.50   e

2.51   f

2.52   b

2.53   d

2.54   √ foreign affairs
√ treasury
√ war
√ attorney general

2.55   Judiciary Act

2.56   National Bank
excise taxes
the issuance of government bonds

2.57   Any order: Democratic-Republicans; Federalists

2.58   weak

SECTION 3

3.1   sectionalism

3.2   deem

3.3   the Supreme Court could declare acts of Congress unconstitutional

3.4   the Revolution of 1800

3.5   eliminated internal excise taxes

3.6   Aaron Burr

3.7   modified voting restrictions

3.8   the closing of the port of New Orleans to American traffic

3.9   James Monroe

3.10   false

3.11   true

3.12   false

3.13   false

3.14   true

3.15   Any four of the following; Any order:
a. Monroe Doctrine
b. increased importance of the Supreme Court in the Federal government
c. Marshall's broad interpretation of the Constitution
d. President Monroe's travels throughout the country
or A protective tariff was passed

3.16   initiate

3.17   industrialized

3.18   Missouri

3.19   Thomas Jefferson
3.20   state
3.21   true
3.22   true
3.23   false
3.24   true
3.25   false
3.26   true
3.27   c. owning property
3.28   a. laborers
3.29   c. fewer Indians and indentured servants
        were available
3.30   b. the Atlantic Triangle
3.31   c. freed in return for their military service
3.32   farming
3.33   Slavery
3.34   c
3.35   a
3.36   e
3.37   f
3.38   b
3.39   d
3.40   false
3.41   true
3.42   false
3.43   false
3.44   true
3.45   1865
3.46   Civil Rights
3.47   grandfather clause
3.48   independence
3.49   a. the Spanish Ambassador wrote an
            insulting letter about McKinley
        b. explosion of the battleship Maine in
            Havana harbor
3.50   a. United States
        b. Spain
3.51   true
3.52   false
3.53   false
3.54   true
3.55   false

SECTION 4
4.1   defray
4.2   component
4.3   Examples: abundant raw materials, river
        ways to transport raw materials and
        finished goods, inventions to make
        manufacturing and communication easier,
        vast labor supply including immigrants
        needing work, wars of 1800s had spurred
        production of military goods.

4.4   d
4.5   c
4.6   e
4.7   f
4.8   g
4.9   b
4.10   a
4.11   corporations
4.12   stockholders
4.13   monopolies
4.14   Federal Trade Commission,Clayton Anti-
        Trust Act
4.15   unions
4.16   National Labor Union
4.17   American Federation of Labor
4.18   b
4.19   c
4.20   a
4.21   Example:
        The United States could not allow its ships
        to be attacked by the Germans. The
        United States was trying to remain
        neutral in the war and was trying to carry
        on trade as usual. It could not allow itself
        to be attacked without retaliating.
4.22   Any order:
        a. overconfidence in the nation's
            prosperity
        b. large industries not as successful as
            they appeared
        c. farmers producing more than they
            could sell
        d. competition from foreign countries
        e. United States extending loans to
            foreign countries for the purchase of its
            products
        f. people buying too much on credit
        g. speculative buying on the stock market
4.23   d
4.24   a
4.25   b
4.26   c
4.27   Franklin D. Roosevelt
4.28   √ to cure the injustices within the business
            and the financial communities
        √ to give relief to labor and to agricultural
            groups
4.29   √ Federal Emergency Relief Act
        √ The Social Security Act
        √ Emergency Banking Act
        √ The Agricultural Adjustment Act

SECTION 5

5.1	surveillance
5.2	Any order:
	built up Germany's military
	invaded Poland
	invaded Austria
	invaded Czechoslovakia
5.3	false
5.4	true
5.5	false
5.6	true
5.7	true
5.8	false
5.9	true
5.10	b
5.11	d
5.12	e
5.13	c
5.14	a
5.15	c
5.16	true
5.17	false
5.18	Paris
5.19	20,000
5.20	predicate
5.21	implicated
5.22	Alliance for Progress
5.23	b
5.24	Poverty
5.25	railroad
5.26	Great Society
5.27	Medicare
5.28	a. bombing
	b. North Vietnam
5.29	Examples: overrode his veto of a resolution to limit Presidential war powers, investigation of Watergate, impeachment recommendations.
5.30	√ Nixon Doctrine
	√ Visit to China
5.31	√ Price Commission
	√ draft lottery
	√ Environmental Protection Agency
5.32	Examples: established council on wage and price stability, proposed tax increases for corporations and citizens.
5.33	inflation
5.34	pardon
5.35	true
5.36	false
5.37	true
5.38	false

5.39	true
5.40	d
5.41	a
5.42	e
5.43	b
5.44	f
5.45	c
5.46	false
5.47	false
5.48	true
5.49	true
5.50	true
5.51	false
5.52	true
5.53	true
5.54	false
5.55	true
5.56	false
5.57	false
5.58	true
5.59	false
5.60	false
5.61	true

SECTION 6

6.1	Christa McAuliffe
6.2	Hubble Telescope
6.3	Afghanistan
6.4	Grenada
6.5	George W. Bush
6.6	Hurricane Katrina
6.7	Manuel Noriega
6.8	true
6.9	false
6.10	true
6.11	false
6.12	b
6.13	c
6.14	c
6.15	b
6.16	c
6.17	d
6.18	a
6.19	d
6.20	b
6.21	a
6.22	b

SELF TEST 1

1.01	true
1.02	true
1.03	true
1.04	false
1.05	false
1.06	true
1.07	false
1.08	true
1.09	true
1.010	true
1.011	true
1.012	clergy/clergymen; landowners/lords; peasants/serfs
1.013	Marco Polo
1.014	Johann Gutenberg
1.015	bourgeoisie
1.016	200
1.017	trade
1.018	colonies; import
1.019	a, b, d
1.020	a
1.021	a, c, d
1.022	d
1.023	d
1.024	a

SELF TEST 2

2.01	true
2.02	false
2.03	true
2.04	true
2.05	false
2.06	b
2.07	c
2.08	a
2.09	b
2.010	d
2.011	a
2.012	d
2.013	a
2.014	c
2.015	b
2.016	Sir Walter Raleigh
2.017	Virginia Dare
2.018	John Smith
2.019	John Rolfe
2.020	indentured
2.021	1619
2.022	Calvin; Luther
2.023	Sir Francis Drake
2.024	a
2.025	f
2.026	i
2.027	b
2.028	e
2.029	g
2.030	c
2.031	d
2.032	h

SELF TEST 3

3.01	h
3.02	f
3.03	g
3.04	a
3.05	c
3.06	d
3.07	b
3.08	e
3.09	Richard Hakluyt
3.010	fall line
3.011	Roger Williams
3.012	Thomas Hooker
3.013	proprietary
3.014	Catholics; Lord Baltimore
3.015	New York
3.016	New Jersey
3.017	Africa
3.018	Georgia
3.019	b, d, g, h
3.020	a, c, e, f
3.021	a, b, c
3.022	d, e
3.023	c
3.024	false
3.025	false
3.026	false

SELF TEST 1

1.01	True
1.02	False
1.03	True
1.04	False
1.05	True
1.06	True
1.07	c
1.08	b
1.09	a
1.010	e
1.011	d
1.012	Boston Tea Party
1.013	Sons of Liberty
1.014	mercantile (mercantilism)
1.015	Rights and Grievances
1.016	James Otis
1.017	Townshend
1.018	'Sugar Act"
	"Molasses Act"
	"Wool Act"
	"Hat Act"
	"Tea Tax"
	"Stamp Act"
	"Iron Act"
1.019	First Continental Congress
1.020	b, e, f and g
1.021	c
1.022	d
1.023	b
1.024	d
1.025	b and c
1.026	3
1.027	4
1.028	2
1.029	5
1.030	1

SELF TEST 2

2.01	True
2.02	False
2.03	False
2.04	False
2.05	False
2.06	True
2.07	False
2.08	True
2.09	True
2.010	b
2.011	i
2.012	f
2.013	h
2.014	a
2.015	c
2.016	j
2.017	d
2.018	g
2.019	e
2.020	d
2.021	c
2.022	c and d
2.023	a, b, c and d
2.024	a and d
2.025	a and d
2.026	a and b
2.027	Cornwallis
2.028	Benjamin Franklin
2.029	Declaration of Independence
2.030	Patrick Henry
2.031	f
2.032	d
2.033	e
2.034	c
2.035	b
2.036	a

SELF TEST 3

3.01	True
3.02	True
3.03	True
3.04	True
3.05	False
3.06	True
3.07	True
3.08	True
3.09	True
3.010	100,000
3.011	Federalists
3.012	Antifederalists
3.013	checks and balances
3.014	Patrick Henry
3.015	French
3.016	Bill of Rights
3.017	Baron von Steuben
3.018	Mississippi River; British
3.019	Thomas Paine
3.020	Intolerable; Boston
3.021	c, d, f and g
3.022	a, b, d
3.023	b
3.024	c

SELF TEST 1

1.01	true
1.02	true
1.03	false
1.04	true
1.05	false
1.06	true
1.07	false
1.08	c
1.09	c
1.010	d
1.011	d
1.012	a
1.013	d
1.014	c
1.015	b
1.016	a
1.017	b
1.018	c
1.019	a
1.020	g
1.021	h
1.022	e
1.023	d
1.024	f
1.025	a
1.026	c
1.027	f
1.028	b
1.029	d
1.030	e
1.031	French; ships
1.032	money
1.033	Kentucky;Virginia
1.034	Federalist

SELF TEST 2

2.01	d
2.02	a
2.03	d
2.04	a
2.05	b
2.06	d
2.07	c
2.08	true
2.09	true
2.010	false
2.011	true
2.012	false
2.013	true
2.014	false
2.015	h
2.016	d
2.017	k
2.018	e
2.019	l
2.020	j
2.021	i
2.022	c
2.023	f
2.024	b
2.025	a
2.026	g
2.027	All boundaries were restored to their pre-war locations and the two nations agreed to stop fighting.

SELF TEST 3

3.01	d
3.02	d
3.03	c
3.04	d
3.05	d
3.06	b
3.07	a
3.08	b, c
3.09	true
3.010	false
3.011	true
3.012	true
3.013	false
3.014	true
3.015	Monroe Doctrine
3.016	internal improvements (roads and canals)
3.017	8; 90%
3.018	h
3.019	c
3.020	a
3.021	i
3.022	b
3.023	k
3.024	g
3.025	e
3.026	d
3.027	j
3.028	f

SELF TEST 1

1.01	false
1.02	false
1.03	false
1.04	false
1.05	false
1.06	false
1.07	true
1.08	false
1.09	false
1.010	d
1.011	c
1.012	c
1.013	b
1.014	d
1.015	h
1.016	g
1.017	j
1.018	e
1.019	a
1.020	i
1.021	c
1.022	f
1.023	b
1.024	d
1.025	Northeast
1.026	Britain
1.027	boundary
1.028	Dred Scott
1.029	Maine
1.030	loyalty; Mexican
1.031	Wilmot
1.032	Freeport Doctrine
1.033	tariffs
1.034	slavery
1.035	slavery
1.036	Abomination

SELF TEST 2

2.01	false
2.02	false
2.03	true
2.04	false
2.05	false
2.06	true
2.07	false
2.08	false
2.09	true
2.010	b
2.011	c
2.012	d
2.013	a
2.014	d
2.015	g
2.016	a
2.017	b
2.018	i
2.019	h
2.020	e
2.021	c
2.022	d
2.023	j
2.024	f
2.025	b, c, e
2.026	craftsman
2.027	Dred Scott
2.028	*The Liberator*
2.029	boundary
2.030	Harriet Tubman
2.031	Manifest Destiny

SELF TEST 1

1.01   c
1.02   d
1.03   b
1.04   e
1.05   f
1.06   a
1.07   i
1.08   k
1.09   j
1.010 l
1.011 g
1.012 h
1.013 g
1.014 f
1.015 h
1.016 e
1.017 c
1.018 a
1.019 d
1.020 b
1.021 a, c, e
1.022 b
1.023 c
1.024 a
1.025 d
1.026 b
1.027 a
1.028 c
1.029 a
1.030 true
1.031 false

SELF TEST 2

2.01   false
2.02   true
2.03   false
2.04   false
2.05   true
2.06   true
2.07   true
2.08   b
2.09   c
2.010 c
2.011 a
2.012 b
2.013 b
2.014 a
2.015 f
2.016 e
2.017 d
2.018 c
2.019 j
2.020 i
2.021 h
2.022 g
2.023 Richmond; Virginia
2.024 Ulysses S. Grant
2.025 cotton
2.026 Vicksburg; Gettysburg
2.027 Stephen Douglas
2.028 divide and conquer

SELF TEST 3

3.01   c
3.02   d
3.03   b
3.04   b
3.05   a
3.06   b
3.07   c
3.08   c
3.09   d
3.010 g
3.011 e
3.012 a
3.013 h
3.014 i
3.015 f
3.016 k
3.017 l
3.018 b
3.019 j
3.020 1861; 1865
3.021 oath; readmitted
3.022 Appomattox Court House
3.023 John Wilkes Booth; Ford's Theater
3.024 Andrew Johnson
3.025 Black Codes
3.026 Tennessee
3.027 d
3.028 e
3.029 j
3.030 f
3.031 g
3.032 k
3.033 h
3.034 a
3.035 i
3.036 b
3.037 c

SELF TEST 1

1.01	b
1.02	a
1.03	e
1.04	f
1.05	c
1.06	d
1.07	i
1.08	j
1.09	g
1.010	h
1.011	b
1.012	c
1.013	e
1.014	a
1.015	d
1.016	e
1.017	d
1.018	b
1.019	c
1.020	a
1.021	false
1.022	false
1.023	true
1.024	true
1.025	false
1.026	true
1.027	true
1.028	true
1.029	true
1.030	true
1.031	false
1.032	true
1.033	true
1.034	false
1.035	true
1.036	workers; capital; natural resources
1.037	a, b, c, d
1.038	a, b, c, e
1.039	a, b, d, e
1.040	a, c, d, e
1.041	a, b, c, e, f

SELF TEST 2

2.01	b
2.02	c
2.03	d
2.04	h
2.05	j
2.06	i
2.07	a
2.08	f
2.09	e
2.010	g
2.011	Model T; assembly line
2.012	capital; government
2.013	tenements; factories
2.014	paid less
2.015	a, b, c, e, f
2.016	a, c, d
2.017	a, b, c, d, f
2.018	a, b, c, d, e
2.019	a, c, d, e
2.020	a, c, d, e, f
2.021	c
2.022	a, c, e
2.023	b, c, d
2.024	c, d, e
2.025	true
2.026	false
2.027	false
2.028	true
2.029	false
2.030	true
2.031	false
2.032	true
2.033	false
2.034	true
2.035	true

SELF TEST 3

3.01	g
3.02	f
3.03	j
3.04	i
3.05	d
3.06	a
3.07	c
3.08	b
3.09	h
3.010	e
3.011	i
3.012	h
3.013	f
3.014	e
3.015	c
3.016	a
3.017	j
3.018	g
3.019	b
3.020	d
3.021	true
3.022	true
3.023	false

3.024 true
3.025 false
3.026 false
3.027 true
3.028 true
3.029 true
3.030 true
3.031 a, b, c, e
3.032 a, b, d
3.033 a, b, c, d
3.034 a, c, d
3.035 a, b, d, f

SELF TEST 4
4.01 b
4.02 a
4.03 g
4.04 f
4.05 k
4.06 j
4.07 d
4.08 i
4.09 h
4.010 e
4.011 n
4.012 l
4.013 c
4.014 o
4.015 m
4.016 urbanization
4.017 corporation
4.018 Agricultural
4.019 Triple Entente
4.020 Triple Alliance
4.021 Boxer Rebellion
4.022 Monroe Doctrine
4.023 collective bargaining
4.024 Big Stick Policy
4.025 true
4.026 false
4.027 false
4.028 false
4.029 true
4.030 true
4.031 true
4.032 false
4.033 true
4.034 true
4.035 false
4.036 a
4.037 b

4.038 a, b, d, e, f
4.039 a, b, d, e, f
4.040 a, b, c, e
4.041 b, c, d
4.042 a, c, d, e
4.043 Entente
4.044 Alliance
4.045 The lure of factory salaries drew many; the attractiveness of cultural, educational and recreational advantages drew others; also a desire to strike it rich like some had brought many to the city.
4.046 newly acquired possessions making U.S. reach out; involvement spread to the Far East; Roosevelt became involved in peace talks between many nations.

SELF TEST 1

1.01	g
1.02	a
1.03	b
1.04	j
1.05	f
1.06	e
1.07	i
1.08	h
1.09	c
1.010	d
1.011	j
1.012	d
1.013	c
1.014	f
1.015	i
1.016	a
1.017	h
1.018	b
1.019	e
1.020	g
1.021	true
1.022	false
1.023	true
1.024	true
1.025	false
1.026	false
1.027	true
1.028	true
1.029	false
1.030	true
1.031	d
1.032	e
1.033	c
1.034	f
1.035	d
1.036	United States Citizens

SELF TEST 2

2.01	d
2.02	j
2.03	a
2.04	i
2.05	g
2.06	h
2.07	c
2.08	b
2.09	f
2.010	e
2.011	i
2.012	e
2.013	f
2.014	h
2.015	g
2.016	a
2.017	b
2.018	k
2.019	c
2.020	d
2.021	j
2.022	true
2.023	false
2.024	true
2.025	false
2.026	true
2.027	false
2.028	true
2.029	true
2.030	true
2.031	true
2.032	d
2.033	c
2.034	a
2.035	e
2.036	d
2.037	d
2.038	b
2.039	crime
2.040	People were weary of fighting for causes and campaigns; they wanted to center their interest on their own betterment.

SELF TEST 3

3.01	Woodrow Wilson
3.02	Charles G. Dawes
3.03	Warren G. Harding
3.04	Karl Marx
3.05	internationalism
3.06	Stalin
3.07	isolationism
3.08	urbanization
3.09	Eighteenth Amendment
3.010	Treaty of Versailles
3.011	private sector
3.012	true
3.013	true
3.014	true
3.015	true
3.016	true
3.017	false
3.018	false
3.019	e
3.020	a
3.021	i

3.022 d
3.023 j
3.024 g
3.025 c
3.026 f
3.027 h
3.028 b
3.029 a, b, c, d, f
3.030 a, c, d, e
3.031 a, b, c, e
3.032 b, c, d
3.033 a, c, d

SELF TEST 4
4.01 c
4.02 d
4.03 b
4.04 h
4.05 i
4.06 a
4.07 k
4.08 j
4.09 g
4.010 e
4.011 f
4.012 a
4.013 e
4.014 b
4.015 d
4.016 c
4.017 true
4.018 true
4.019 true
4.020 true
4.021 false
4.022 false
4.023 true
4.024 true
4.025 a, c, e
4.026 His early struggles with polio taught him determination to win over high obstacles. His political experience gave him insight into national problems. His character and love for America were advantages.

SELF TEST 1

1.01	e
1.02	f
1.03	a
1.04	b
1.05	g
1.06	h
1.07	i
1.08	c
1.09	d
1.010	j
1.011	true
1.012	false
1.013	false
1.014	false
1.015	false
1.016	true
1.017	true
1.018	true
1.019	false
1.020	true
1.021	military
1.022	Great Depression
1.023	Ethiopia
1.024	France, USA, Russia
1.025	Dwight D. Eisenhower
1.026	Soviets
1.027	Corregidor
1.028	MacArthur
1.029	Kamikaze
1.030	Nagasaki
1.031	d
1.032	b
1.033	a
1.034	c
1.035	b
1.036	a
1.037	a, c
1.038	a
1.039	The Allies drove the Germans and Italians from North Africa; then they swept through Italy, overpowering them; next the Normandy invasion began a successful drive across France into Germany with the Soviets closing in from the east and Allies on the west.

SELF TEST 2

2.01	d
2.02	a
2.03	f
2.04	j
2.05	g
2.06	e
2.07	i
2.08	b
2.09	c
2.010	h
2.011	d
2.012	c
2.013	f
2.014	b
2.015	h
2.016	g
2.017	a
2.018	i
2.019	e
2.020	false
2.021	true
2.022	true
2.023	true
2.024	false
2.025	true
2.026	true
2.027	false
2.028	true
2.029	false
2.030	e
2.031	c
2.032	a, b, c, e
2.033	a
2.034	a
2.035	a
2.036	communism
2.037	Harry S. Truman

SELF TEST 3

3.01	g
3.02	b
3.03	l
3.04	d
3.05	h
3.06	k
3.07	c
3.08	j
3.09	i
3.010	e
3.011	a
3.012	m
3.013	f
3.014	n
3.015	g
3.016	a
3.017	c

3.018   i
3.019   e
3.020   h
3.021   b
3.022   d
3.023   f
3.024   true
3.025   false
3.026   true
3.027   true
3.028   true
3.029   true
3.030   true
3.031   true
3.032   e
3.033   a
3.034   a
3.035   4
3.036   3
3.037   1
3.038   5
3.039   2
3.040   2
3.041   5
3.042   3
3.043   1
3.044   4
3.045   6
3.046   Answer includes: Established the Peace
        Corps, sent military advisors to South
        Vietnam, effectively stopped the build-up
        of Soviet missiles in Cuba.

SELF TEST 1

1.01	h
1.02	j
1.03	a
1.04	f
1.05	b
1.06	e
1.07	g
1.08	d
1.09	i
1.010	c
1.011	cosmonaut
1.012	Berlin Wall
1.013	containment
1.014	Peace Corps
1.015	1961, 1989
1.016	1999
1.017	true
1.018	true
1.019	false
1.020	true
1.021	false
1.022	b
1.023	b
1.024	d
1.025	a
1.026	d
1.027	h
1.028	e
1.029	f
1.030	g
1.031	c
1.032	b

SELF TEST 2

2.01	3
2.02	5
2.03	2
2.04	1
2.05	6
2.06	4
2.07	d
2.08	e
2.09	c
2.010	g
2.011	b
2.012	a
2.013	f
2.014	a, c, d, f
2.015	b, d, e
2.016	twenty-one, eighteen
2.017	Gerald Ford
2.018	Henry Kissinger
2.019	Vietnamization
2.020	pardon
2.021	abortion
2.022	true
2.023	false
2.024	false
2.025	false
2.026	true
2.027	true
2.028	d
2.029	a
2.030	g
2.031	b
2.032	f
2.033	h
2.034	c
2.035	e

SELF TEST 3

3.01	d
3.02	b
3.03	j
3.04	g
3.05	e
3.06	f
3.07	a
3.08	c
3.09	h
3.010	i
3.011	a, b, e, g, h
3.012	Sandra Day O'Connor
3.013	Geraldine Ferraro
3.014	Columbia, Challenger
3.015	Reaganomics
3.016	Nicaragua
3.017	Ronald Reagan
3.018	Republican
3.019	false
3.020	false
3.021	true
3.022	true
3.023	true
3.024	false
3.025	true
3.026	Grenada
3.027	Boris Yeltsin
3.028	Persian Gulf War

3.029   Bosnia
3.030   100
3.031   Saddam Hussein
3.032   false
3.033   true
3.034   true
3.035   true
3.036   true

SELF TEST 4
4.01   a
4.02   h
4.03   f
4.04   g
4.05   i
4.06   d
4.07   b
4.08   e
4.09   c
4.010   a. Indian
4.011   c. Osama bin Laden
4.012   c. The Sears Tower in Chicago
4.013   true
4.014   false
4.015   true

SELF TEST 1

1.01	false
1.02	true
1.03	false
1.04	true
1.05	true
1.06	false
1.07	false
1.08	true
1.09	true
1.010	Any order: serfs, noblemen ,clergy
1.011	Any two:
	increasing power of middle class
	the Crusades
	trade encouraged serfs to leave manors
1.012	Muslims
1.013	astrolabe
1.014	mercantilism
1.015	Either order:
	internal struggles
	the threat of Spain
1.016	Reformation
1.017	Any two of the following: Quakers, Puritans, Separatists, Pilgrims, Catholics
1.018	raw materials
1.019	Toleration Act
1.020	f
1.021	d
1.022	b
1.023	h
1.024	g
1.025	a
1.026	c
1.027	e
1.028	j
1.029	i

SELF TEST 2

2.01	true
2.02	false
2.03	true
2.04	true
2.05	true
2.06	false
2.07	true
2.08	which country controlled the North American continent
2.09	restrict manufacturing in the colonies
2.010	settle anywhere other than the land along the Atlantic Coast
2.011	collection of taxes
2.012	with "The Great Compromise"
2.013	it divides power between the federal and the state governments
2.014	Common Sense
2.015	boycotting
2.016	Yorktown
2.017	√ establish a national bank system
	√ place excise taxes on certain goods for government operating money
	√ government assume states' war debts
	√ established a method of issuing of government bonds
2.018	√ Declaration of Independence
	√ Stamp Act
	√ Intolerable Acts
	√ fighting in Boston
2.019	b
2.020	d
2.021	f
2.022	h
2.023	j
2.024	k
2.025	i
2.026	g
2.027	e
2.028	c
2.029	a

SELF TEST 3

3.01	false
3.02	true
3.03	true
3.04	false
3.05	true
3.06	true
3.07	false
3.08	false
3.09	true
3.010	the Atlantic Triangle
3.011	Underground Railroad
3.012	slave codes
3.013	Manifest Destiny
3.014	South Carolina
3.015	Jefferson Davis
3.016	Richmond, Virginia
3.017	the Union blockade
3.018	John Wilkes Booth
3.019	Freedman's Bureau
3.020	skilled laborers
3.021	abolished slavery forever
3.022	divided all Confederate states into five military districts
3.023	all of the above

3.024	instituted poll taxes and literacy tests	4.014	i
3.025	*Common Sense*	4.015	k
3.026	Thomas Jefferson	4.016	m
3.027	*Marbury vs. Madison*	4.017	o
3.028	New Orleans	4.018	a
3.029	New Orleans	4.019	n
3.030	Sectionalism	4.020	l
3.031	Any three:	4.021	j
	protective tariff	4.022	h
	westward expansion	4.023	f
	internal improvements	4.024	d
	slavery	4.025	b
3.032	a. share	4.026	c
	b. government	4.027	b
3.033	Any order:	4.028	c
	the impressment of sailors	4.029	a
	British interference with the United States	4.030	b
	inciting Indian warfare	4.031	d
3.034	Either order:	4.032	b
	explosion of the battleship *Maine* in	4.033	b
	Havana harbor	4.034	a
	the Spanish ambassador wrote an	4.035	d
	insulting letter about President McKinley	4.036	c
3.035	b	4.037	a
3.036	d	4.038	c
3.037	f	4.039	b
3.038	h	4.040	d
3.039	j	4.041	c
3.040	l	4.042	governmental
3.041	n		private business
3.042	a	4.043	withdrawals
3.043	o	4.044	steamboat
3.044	m	4.045	Any order:
3.045	k		a. natural resources
3.046	i		b. raw materials
3.047	g		c. labor force
3.048	e		
3.049	c		

SELF TEST 4

SELF TEST 5

4.01	true	5.01	true
4.02	false	5.02	false
4.03	true	5.03	false
4.04	true	5.04	true
4.05	false	5.05	true
4.06	false	5.06	false
4.07	false	5.07	true
4.08	false	5.08	true
4.09	true	5.09	false
4.010	true	5.010	false
4.011	c	5.011	true
4.012	e	5.012	f
4.013	g	5.013	d
		5.014	b
		5.015	h

5.016 i

5.017 j

5.018 g

5.019 a

5.020 c

5.021 e

5.022 d

5.023 d

5.024 c

5.025 b

5.026 c

5.027 a

5.028 c

5.029 b

5.030 c

5.031 Two causes of World War II were military build up and Hitler's invasion of small countries.

5.032 Pearl Harbor

5.033 Any order:
Germany
Japan
Italy

5.034 Any order:
United States
Britain
Soviet Union

5.035 withdrawal

5.036 James E. Carter

5.037 resigned

5.038 c

5.039 a

5.040 e

5.041 g

5.042 i

5.043 k

5.044 m

5.045 o

5.046 n

5.047 l

5.048 j

5.049 h

5.050 f

5.051 b

5.052 d

5.053 c

5.054 e

5.055 g

5.056 i

5.057 k

5.058 m

5.059 o

5.060 a

5.061 n

5.062 l

5.063 j

5.064 h

5.065 f

5.066 d

5.067 b

SELF TEST 6

6.01 1981

6.02 *Columbia*

6.03 Hubble

6.04 a. Christa McAuliffe
b. *Challenger*

6.05 Richard Nixon

6.06 al Qaeda

6.07 Southern

6.08 d

6.09 b

6.010 c

6.011 d

6.012 c

6.013 b

6.014 b

6.015 b

6.016 d

6.017 h

6.018 f

6.019 i

6.020 a

6.021 c

6.022 e

6.023 g

6.024 false

6.025 true

6.026 true

6.027 false

6.028 true

6.029 true

6.030 true

6.031 true

6.032 false

6.033 true

1.   True

2.   True

3.   True

4.   False

5.   True

6.   False

7.   False

8.   True

9.   True

10.   c

11.   i

12.   g

13.   d

14.   f

15.   h

16.   b

17.   a

18.   j

19.   e

20.   d

21.   c

22.   a

23.   c

24.   a, c, d

25.   a, b, c

26.   d, e

27.   200

28.   Calvin; Luther

29.   Sir Francis Drake

30.   To have a colony south of the Carolinas that
        would serve as a buffer to keep the Spanish
        from moving further northward; to provide
        a home and a new life for British prisoners
        and convicts.

1. True

2. False

3. True

4. False

5. False

6. True

7. True

8. i

9. b

10. j

11. d

12. g

13. a

14. f

15. c

16. e

17. h

18. a and d

19. b, c and d

20. c

21. a

22. b

23. a

24. c

25. a

26. b

27. c

28. b

29. a

30. c

31. a

32. Senate; House of Representatives

33. legislative, executive and judicial; checks, balances

34. government

35. foreign soil

1. c
2. c
3. c
4. b
5. b
6. c
7. b
8. b
9. d
10. c
11. d
12. b
13. James Monroe; Robert Livingston
14. true
15. true
16. true
17. true
18. false
19. true
20. true
21. true
22. true
23. false
24. true
25. true
26. false
27. false
28. true
29. true
30. false
31. true
32. e
33. j

34. c
35. b
36. i
37. l
38. d
39. k
40. g
41. a
42. h
43. f

1. true

2. false

3. true

4. true

5. false

6. false

7. true

8. true

9. a, c, f

10. b, c, e

11. newspapers

12. Stephen Douglas; Abraham Lincoln

13. Bleeding Kansas

14. a

15. c

16. d

17. d

18. l

19. e

20. c

21. j

22. a

23. k

24. f

25. g

26. b

27. n

28. i

29. h

30. m

1. true
2. true
3. false
4. true
5. true
6. true
7. false
8. false
9. true
10. true
11. false
12. false
13. true
14. false
15. false
16. true
17. false
18. d
19. i
20. j
21. f
22. e
23. g
24. h
25. b
26. c
27. a
28. g
29. j
30. f
31. i
32. d
33. e

34. h
35. c
36. b
37. a
38. c
39. d
40. i
41. f
42. h
43. a
44. j
45. g
46. b
47. e
48. Ulysses S. Grant
49. Robert E. Lee

1.	b	35.	a, b, c, e
2.	e	36.	a, b, d, e
3.	l	37.	a, b, c, d
4.	c	38.	a, b, c, f
5.	i	39.	a, b, d
6.	d	40.	a, c, d, e
7.	f		
8.	k		
9.	g		
10.	a		
11.	j		
12.	h		

41. Strong nationalism led to so much national pride that negotiations became impossible; imperialism often ended in nations squabbling or fighting over desirable conquests.

13. assembly line
14. Agricultural
15. collective bargaining
16. nationalism
17. imperialism
18. monopoly
19. urbanization
20. Monroe Doctrine
21. Triple Entente
22. Open Door Policy
23. Spanish-American War
24. isolationism
25. false
26. true
27. true
28. true
29. false
30. true
31. false
32. false
33. true
34. true

1. e
2. l
3. d
4. f
5. k
6. c
7. g
8. b
9. h
10. j
11. a
12. i
13. Fourteen Points
14. Pershing
15. Treaty of Versailles
16. League of Nations
17. urbanization
18. progressivism
19. internationalism
20. isolationism
21. prohibition
22. Ku Klux Klan
23. true
24. true
25. true
26. false
27. true
28. true
29. true
30. true
31. true
32. true

33. c, e
34. f, h, i, j
35. a, g
36. k, l, m
37. b, d
38. a, b, c, e
39. d
40. c
41. a
42. e

43. His early struggles with polio taught him determination to win over high obstacles. His political experience gave him insight into national problems. His character and love for America were advantages.

1. c

2. a

3. b

4. j

5. f

6. d

7. e

8. l

9. i

10. g

11. h

12. k

13. true

14. true

15. false

16. true

17. true

18. true

19. false

20. true

21. false

22. true

23. mobilization

24. Vietnam

25. Pacific

26. Johnson

27. Nixon

28. Allied, World War II

29. Axis

30. Eisenhower

31. protest

32. a, b, c, e, f

33. a, b, c, e

34. a, b, c, d, f

35. d

36. c

37. Answer should include: persuade other countries to their way of thinking, the U.S. wanted to give aid to other countries to resist Communism, Soviet Union wanted a forceful takeover of other countries.

1. b
2. a
3. e
4. d
5. h
6. g
7. f
8. c
9. b
10. c
11. a
12. a
13. c
14. c
15. e
16. d
17. f
18. g
19. h
20. true
21. false
22. false
23. true
24. false
25. true
26. a, b, d, e, g, h
27. 18
28. Columbia
29. Reaganomics
30. Star Wars
31. Arkansas

1.	true		37.	Great Compromise
2.	false		38.	Watergate
3.	true		39.	*Marbury v. Madison*
4.	false		40.	Union Blockade
5.	false		41.	South Carolina
6.	false		42.	Underground Railroad
7.	true		43.	League of Nations
8.	true		44.	Gerald Ford
9.	true		45.	James E. Carter
10.	false		46.	resigned
11.	a		47.	Carter
12.	c		48.	New Orleans
13.	a		49.	September 11, 2001
14.	d		50.	Iraq
15.	b		51.	b
16.	c		52.	d
17.	b		53.	g
18.	c		54.	f
19.	c		55.	e
20.	b		56.	c
21.	h		57.	a
22.	j		58.	i
23.	l		59.	k
24.	n		60.	m
25.	o		61.	o
26.	m		63.	n
27.	k		63.	l
28.	i		64.	j
29.	a		65.	h
30.	c			
31.	e			
32.	g			
33.	f			
34.	d			
35.	b			
36.	Any order: clergy noblemen serfs			

1. false

2. true

3. true

4. true

5. false

6. false

7. true

8. true

9. false

10. true

11. b

12. c

13. b

14. b

15. c

16. a

17. a

18. b

19. b

20. g

21. f

22. b

23. a

24. c

25. e

26. Jamestown

27. Duke of York

28. Massachusetts Bay

29. Maryland

30. Rhode Island

31. Connecticut

32. proprietary

33. eight

34. Society of Friends or Quakers

35. Georgia

1. true

2. true

3. false

4. false

5. true

6. true

7. true

8. true

9. true

10. Thomas Paine

11. Washington

12. French

13. independence

14. Yorktown

15. the Mississippi River

16. slavery

17. Federalists

18. Western land

19. Articles of Confederation

20. Northwest Ordinance

21. Example:
Rivalry among the states over the apportionment of representation to the government

22. The Constitution did not provide guarantees of individual rights.

23. Opponents of the new Constitution feared a strong central government.

24. Example:
The Great Compromise created a two house Congress made up of a Senate and a House of Representatives. House members were to be allotted on the basis of population and in the Senate, states would have equal representation.

25. i

26. f

27. g

28. a

29. j

30. h

31. b

32. k

33. e

34. d

35. Example; any order:
   a. Congress had no power to collect taxes.
   b. Congress had no power to control trade.
   c. No system of national courts
      Equal voting power led to jealousies between states.

36. Any order:
   a. Executive
   b. Legislative
   c. Judicial

1. false

2. true

3. true

4. true

5. false

6. true

7. true

8. true

9. true

10. true

11. Examples; any order:
    a. The United States will not interfere in European wars,
    b. The United States will not interfere with current colonies,
    c. The American continents are not open for European colonization and
    d. Any attempt to colonize in this hemisphere would be a threat to the U.S.

12. increased

13. Jeffersonian Era

14. cabinet

15. Any order:
    a. Hamilton
    b. Jefferson
    c. Madison

16. Twelfth Amendment

17. Lewis and Clark

18. limited government

19. Britain

20. South

21. Alexander Hamilton

22. Democrat Republican or Republican Party

23. Federalist Party

24. Twelfth Amendment

25. War of 1812

26. Erie Canal

27. Missouri Compromise

28. spoils system

29. c

30. g

31. f

32. h

33. b

34. a

35. e

1. false

2. false

3. true

4. false

5. true

6. false

7. false

8. false

9. false

10. true

11. Maine

12. slavery

13. popular sovereignty

14. Any order:
    a. field workers
    b. domestic workers
    c. artisans or craftsmen

15. either *Liberator* or *North Star*

16. Henry Clay

17. roads and canals (internal improvements)

18. the Mexican Cession

19. Oregon

20. Texas

21. Fugitive Slave Act

22. e

23. g

24. h

25. f

26. a

27. b

28. c

1. true
2. false
3. true
4. false
5. false
6. true
7. true
8. true
9. false
10. true
11. c
12. e
13. a
14. f
15. b
16. h
17. i
18. d
19. g
20. l
21. k
22. j
23. b
24. a
25. c
26. d
27. a
28. d
29. b
30. c
31. c
32. a

33. Tenure in Office Act
34. Carpetbaggers
35. (a) Rutherford B. Hayes
    (b) Samuel Tilden
36. Northeast
37. South
38. Any order:
    a. Mississippi
    b. Florida
    c. Louisiana, Texas,
        Georgia or Alabama
39. Vicksburg
40. Andrew Johnson

1. j

2. e

3. f

4. i

5 a

6. l

7. m

8. d

9. b

10. k

11. c

12. g

13. a. cotton gin
    b. reaper

14. a. steamboat
    b steam locomotive

15. telegraph

16. Transatlantic Cable

17. drilled the first oil well

18. Rough Riders

19. Philippines

20. Bismarck

21. Seward's

22. Panama Canal

23. Spanish-American War

24. true

25. false

26. true

27. true

28. true

29. true

30. true

31. false

32. true

33. true

34. d

35. b

36. a

37. b

38. a

39. b

40. Example:
    Strong nationalism gave rise to such intense pride for individual countries that reasonable negotiations became impossible. Imperialism often ended in fighting between European nations over some desirable conquest. Both gave rise to increased friction, leading to militarism and preparation for war.

41. Example:
    Profits were the goal of business; therefore the worker became little more than an easily replaced commodity. He lost his independence, individuality, creativity, gained few benefits, lived and worked in horrible conditions.

1. i
2. e
3. h
4. b
5. a
6. d
7. k
8. m
9. j
10. l
11. c
12. g
13. Wilson's
14. Austrian and Serbia
15. Eighteenth
16. Lusitania
17. Harding
18. President Hoover
19. military equipment
20. Franklin D. Roosevelt
21. General Pershing
22. Triple Entente
23. false
24. true
25. false
26. true
27. true
28. true
29. false
30. true
31. false
32. true
33. d
34. a
35. c

36. b
37. c
38. Example:
    It boosted Allied morale and it supplied needed manpower, food, supplies and military equipment.

39. Example:
    America enjoyed increased prosperity and production in the 1920s. The Great Depression appeared to develop overnight.

1. f

2. b

3. m

4. a

5. l

6. h

7. k

8. c

9. d

10. g

11. j

12. e

13. Pearl Harbor

14. Either order:
   a. Hiroshima
   b. Nagasaki

15. United Nations

16. Communist

17. Vietnam

18. Vietnamization

19. Pusan Perimeter

20. the Cold War

21. President John Kennedy's

22. Any order:
   a. Germany
   b. Italy
   c. Japan

23. Any order:
   a. United States
   b. Great Britain
   c. France or Russia or China

24. true

25. false

26. true

27. false

28. false

29. false

30. true

31. true

32. true

33. true

34. d

35. b

36. a

37. c

38. b

39. Example:
   America attempted to make a strong stand against Communist infiltration by first backing the nationalist leaders, then offering aid and eventually taking over the actual combat involvement.

1. true
2. true
3. false
4. true
5. true
6. false
7. true
8. true
9. false
10. true
11. c
12. e
13. f
14. h
15. a
16. b
17. d
18. i
19. g
20. k
21. inflation
22. impeachment
23. President Ford
24. the *Mayaguez* rescue or the fall of South Vietnam
25. pardon Nixon
26. doves
27. China, Soviet Union
28. Kennedy
29. the Camp David Accords
30. Watergate
31. a
32. c
33. b
34. d
35. c

1. e

2. h

3. j

4. a

5. i

6. m

7. k

8. b

9. p

10. o

11. g

12. n

13. c

14. d

15. f

16. Thomas Jefferson

17. Emancipation

18. telephone

19. Ulysses S. Grant

20. Robert E. Lee

21. New Deal

22. John F. Kennedy

23. printing press

24. the collection of taxes or the lack of federal courts or no control over trade

25. the withdrawal of 25,000 American troops

26. a

27. c

28. b

29. d

30. a

31. b

32. d

33. a

34. c

35. b

36. true

37. false

38. true

39. true

40. false